ONORATO DAMEN

BORDIGA BEYOND THE MYTH

Prometheus Publications

Prometheus Publications

BM CWO London WC1N 3XX
www.leftcom.org
email: uk@leftcom.org

Translated from the Italian by Jock Dominie, Anthony Pace, and Liz
Rayner.
Layout: Roger Martin.
Thanks to all the comrades who proofread and corrected this work.

ISBN: 978-0-9935805-0-5

Contents

To my companion Cecca*
for a whole life lived
in active militancy,
with a modesty equal to her intense activity
and her total fidelity to the cause of socialism

* Francesca Grossi (born Milan 1901), member of the Committee of Intesa of 1925 and wife of Onorato Damen, she was a founder member of the Internationalist Communist Party in Autumn 1943 and remained dedicated to it until her death in Milan in 1996.

Introducing Onorato Damen

In the English-speaking political scene there is still enormous ignorance about the Italian Left and its key role in maintaining and stimulating the reawakening of a wider internationalist communist movement of which the CWO came to be a part. Too often the phrase "Italian Left" is associated with Antonio Gramsci, whose *Prison Writings* have become a favourite in left reformist and academic circles and who is often mistakenly or deliberately portrayed as the founding-figure of the Communist Party of Italy in 1921.[1] Even amongst more politically aware, the Italian Left tends to be regarded exclusively as 'Bordigism'. This is much nearer the truth, in that Amadeo Bordiga emerged as the prime spokesman when the Communist Party of Italy was formed at Livorno in 1921 (where Gramsci never said a word) and was the undoubted political leader in the new Party Executive until his imprisonment in 1923. Seizing the opportunity the Comintern manoeuvred to oust the Left from the Party Executive even though the Left were still the majority in the Party as a whole; amongst them was Onorato Damen.

Damen always recognised the genius and contribution of Bordiga but was not uncritical of some of his tactical and theoretical positions. Even in 1919 he had been critical of the fact that Bordiga put a tactical question of abstaining from parliamentary activity before the need to form a Communist Party. The result was that the Party's formation was delayed until 1921 by which time the "Red Two Years" were over. Damen was also critical of the way Bordiga passively accepted his substitution as leader of the party by Gramsci and Togliatti in 1923 (Gramsci having been groomed in Moscow on how to keep the party in line whilst Bordiga was imprisoned by the Fascists). Damen and others urged Bordiga to fight back and in 1925 formed a Comitato d'Intesa (Committee of Agreement or Entente) to fight "bolshevisation" but when they were told to dissolve it by Gramsci, Bordiga complied, against the opposition of the other signatories.[2]

Ironically all three were to meet again in 1926 as prisoners of the Fascist regime on the remote island of Ustica. Damen arrived first and set up a kind of communist living quarters in an old "saracen tower" (where the population used to hide from Arab slavers). This became the "Villa Damen". When Gramsci arrived with Bordiga a party "school" was set up where Gramsci led on literature and history, Bordiga on science and Damen on Marxist economics. Gramsci mentions this, and what he and Bordiga did, but Damen was perhaps too controversial and politically active a figure to mention in the *Prison Letters*. After all it was only a few months since the Gramsci-Togliatti Executive Committee had sent out orders to all local PCd'I federations that if Damen turned up anywhere his person and his accommodation should be searched and any documents found on him sent to the leadership. The school only lasted 6 weeks before its members were transferred to less congenial surroundings. Within a few years both Damen and Bordiga were expelled from the party they had founded and Bordiga retired from all political activity for a decade and a half. For the next 17 years Damen was to be in and out of prison, once gaining his release after organising a prison riot in Civitavecchia. He did, however, maintain secret contact with the Italian Fraction, of internationalist communists in exile in France and Belgium. Thus, when a new Internationalist Communist Party was formed in 1943 in opposition to the Stalinists and to both sides in the imperialist war he became one of its most militant and public organisers. Bordiga did not join the new Party but from 1945 wrote a column for its paper, *Battaglia Comunista*.

By 1948 however, Bordiga was arguing for a return to the positions of the Party in 1921 even though history had moved on. He even questioned the very formation of the party as premature and seemed to be arguing for purely theoretical work. His document "On Activism" was written against those like Damen who insisted that theory and practice (praxis) were equally impotent if separated. "On Activism" has valid points against the kind of sterile activism we see so much of amongst the so-called Left today but it was not an accurate picture of what Damen and his comrades were arguing. For Damen the party could not be built "just by sitting behind a typewriter" and argued that there had to be an ongoing attempt to reach the wider working class, even in the situation of an apparent capitalist revival. This became one of the bases of the famous split in the Internationalist Communist Party in 1951-2. All the documents in this collection refer to one or other aspect of the differences with the new cult of what we call "late" Bordigism which emerged in the 1950s. The International Communist Party which was founded by Bordiga has endured numerous splits since with each new manifestation claiming to be the authentic "Bordigist" Party.

Fortunately there is no cult of Damen. Yet his life was a remarkable one. He might easily have been shot for mutiny in the First World War. He managed to survive gun battles with Fascists in the early 1920s, could have been done away with in the prison riot of Civitavecchia or by the Stalinists at the end of the Second World War but somehow he survived it all. We hope the translation of this collection of his writings will bring him to a wider audience as part of our work to carry on and develop what we consider to be the real heritage of the internationalist communist left to which he contributed so much.

Communist Workers' Organisation

December 2015

Preface to the New Italian Edition (2009)

The originality and importance of this volume – in a expanded edition including new documents and editorial notes, from the two previous editions: 1971 and 1977, EPI (Editoriale periodici italiani) – mainly lies in the documents that throw permanent light on the distinctive development and perspectives of the "Italian Left" over decades (among the most tragic in modern history) in the history of international communism.

Putting the two names (Damen – Bordiga) together is no accident, but neatly demonstrates a coincidence of ideas and work, as well as heated debates on the different ways to consider these ideas and that work which, in the concerns of both of them, cemented the organisation of the revolutionary party. There is no political dilettantism here, but dialectically unavoidable contradictory positions, trying to find the correct line of theoretical and practical interpretation in the exclusive interest of the revolutionary party.

Gathered here are the most significant critical analyses about the series of divergences that developed in the post-war period – and "exploded" at a certain point – into real disagreement between Bordiga and a group of his supporters, and a number of comrades who were distinguished by their consistently strong political leadership and revolutionary militancy, both before and after the end of the imperialist conflict. Comrades who had held high the banner of the Left, never giving in or abandoning the struggle despite enormously adverse conditions and persecution; comrades who, with commitment and sacrifice, had continued to develop a theoretical elaboration that was not statically contemplative and allowed a minimum of practical activity, in sharp contrast to what Bordiga advised, and gave an example of, in his own conduct. Militants who, though working in the difficult situation of the period, could certainly not be pushed aside with charges as false and politically defamatory, as ... "activism, the historic refuge of the renegade," dictated by the frenzy of their "political and personal electioneering."

The thirtieth anniversary of the death of Onorato Damen has given us the opportunity to reorganise and enrich this collection of writings and documents, with additional explanatory notes and an appendix consisting of new writings, letters etc ... Materials which, taken together, contribute to a critical analysis of the more than questionable views and behaviour which Bordiga demonstrated after his reappearance at the end of the war. His formal declarations of intransigence were accompanied by a claim to represent, in a personal interpretation which brooked no discussion an "invariant" Marxism which threatened to discredit the figure of the still prestigious representative of the Italian left that was Bordiga himself, at least until the mid-twenties. Not only that, but the group that had gathered in the shadow of this new character saw the work they had done so far for to reconstruct the class political organisation taken

9

down a blind alley.

It was down to Onorato Damen, who we will remember as an indomitable communist fighter in every period of his life, to highlight errors in some of Bordiga's political perspectives, to denounce the danger which threatened not only the recently reconstructed party, but also all the theoretical political and organisational heritage of the Italian left: that is to say, the one revolutionary current that had managed to maintain uninterrupted, throughout the longest and most tragic period of the international communist movement's history, its basic theoretical principles and the political praxis which flowed from it.

Remembering Onorato Damen on the Thirtieth Anniversary of his Death

Monte San Pietrangeli (Ascoli Piceno) 4 December 1893 – Milan 14 Oct 1979

"Without the revolutionary party, every revolt will burn itself out within the system."

Onorato Damen was one of the most representative and prestigious figures of the International Communist Left. When still very young, he fought against revisionism in the PSI and the opportunism of Turati, Treves and Modigliani. With the outbreak of World War I, he was sent to the front, and then demoted from sergeant to private and sentenced to two years in military prison for *"public insults against institutions, incitement to desertion and denunciation of the imperialist nature of the war."* Subsequently, he worked for the socialist newspaper *La Lotta* (Struggle) in Fermo, Le Marche; he worked at the Chamber of Labour in Bologna and in the Casa del Popolo of Granarolo as secretary of the municipal committee of the Leagues; secretary of the Chamber of Labour in Pistoia; and he was arrested in 1921. A supporter of the Italian Communist Left, Damen was a member of the abstentionist Fraction of the PSI and then of the Trade Union Central Committee of the Communist Party of Italy (Livorno 1921).

A target of fascist reaction, he was "kidnapped" by the fascists because he refused to recant his "Bolshevik" ideas. Having resumed contact with the Communist Party of Italy, Damen found himself involved in a gunfight in which a fascist was killed. Acquitted of murder, he was imprisoned for three years in Florence. Released, the Communist Party of Italy illegally transferred him to France through the *Bureau Politique* to organise fellow migrants. Director of the weekly *L'Humanité* in Italian, he returned illegally to Italy in 1924 and was elected deputy for the district of Florence. Within the Communist Party of Italy, the rupture between the leadership headed by Gramsci and the Bordigist left was emerging and Damen criticised the degenerate leadership of the party as well as the somewhat passive attitude of Bordiga.

In 1925, Damen was behind — with Repossi and Fortichiari — the establishment of the *Comitato d'Intesa* in defence of the work of the Left and the political foundation upon which the Communist Party was formed in 1921. In 1926, he was confined to Ustica, then arrested and sent back to prison in Florence and included amongst the Florentine Communists on trial for conspiracy against the State. The Special Court sentenced him to 12 years imprisonment, of which seven were served in the penitentiaries of Saluzzo, Pallanza, Civitavecchia (where he led a prison revolt) and Pianosa. In 1929, he was expelled from the Communist Party of Italy which was now in the service of international counter-revolution. Granted amnesty in 1933 as an "unrepentant communist", Damen was confined to five years in Cantù in

Brianza. In late 1935 he was arrested again, and stopped by police several times in 1937 concerning the events in Spain, suspected of spreading "propaganda of the international left opposition against the policy of the Comintern and against Stalinism in Spain" (Source; the fascist police). Arrested at the outbreak of World War II and sent into internal exile, he was released after the fall of Mussolini in July 1943.

Despite everything, Damen managed – by maintaining illegal contacts and never giving up the role of an active militant regardless of all the sacrifices this demanded — to make his crucial contribution to the birth of the Internationalist Communist Party, the only class response to the slaughter of imperialist war which rejected the "defence" of one imperialist power against another. And the few internationalists outside the prisons were in the forefront when, in 1943, the proletariat of the North was set ablaze, spreading illegal leaflets and their first series of *Prometeo* – newspaper of the *Internationalist Communist Party*.

In 1945, Togliatti and the PCI asked the Committee for National Liberation to sentence to death the leaders of our Party, labelled as "Gestapo agents", primarily Onorato Damen (in the meantime our comrades Fausto Atti and Mario Acquaviva were murdered by the henchmen of the Communist Party of Italy). Saved by his unquestionable moral rectitude, acknowledged even among political adversaries, Damen afterwards tirelessly contributed to the leadership of the Internationalist Communist Party, and to the difficult struggle to rebuild the political organisation necessary for the future battles of the revolutionary proletariat.

The present crisis facing capitalism gives Marxism new strength and theoretical vigour. It confirms once again that the world proletariat can only achieve "progress" and "liberation" in the era of imperialist domination through the socialist revolution. The work and teachings of Damen have allowed all of us to resist, to defend and to strengthen the political and organisational foundations of the future international party of the proletariat, capable of merging theory and practice in concrete and decisive political action.

"The fundamental, and most difficult problem for a revolutionary minority to solve is that of its intervention, and to work on the basis of a political platform for a whole historical period, that of capitalism, no matter what the objective conditions may be, including those of war and counter-revolution, to help the working class to rise from a consciousness of its immediate interests to a consciousness of its essence as a historical class antagonistic to capitalism." (Onorato Damen)

Amadeo Bordiga – The Value and Limitations of an Experience in the History of the "Italian Left"

The name and work of Bordiga mark an important moment in the political history of the revolutionary proletariat. The "Italian Left" (see Appendix Two: A Brief History of the Italian Left), as a current of thought and an initial nucleus of revolutionary cadres, is linked to the critical position Bordiga took in the Italian Socialist Party in the period before the First World War. In the immediate postwar period he organised an abstentionist fraction, which led to the first conflict with the policy of the Third International and personally with Comrade Lenin in the debate in the Second Congress of the International.

During the Imola meeting (1920)[3], Bordiga tactically sacrificed his insistence on abstention to allow agreement between the various currents and groups that would merge on the basis of 21 points (of the Communist International) to form the Communist Party at the Congress of Livorno (1921). Given his stature as a fighter and as the most conscious advocate of the need to split the Socialist Party, he thus became the leader of the Communist Party of Italy. But, along with the other representatives of the Left, he was later sacked so the agenda of the new political leadership, imposed in the interests of the Russian state through the Bolshevisation of all the communist parties adhering to the Third International, could be carried out.

Whatever disagreements we may have had and still have, whatever the fights and internal strife — which this book highlights, including, and especially, those that still remain relevant today — we support and defend what belonged to Bordiga and to us, that is to say, the "Italian Left" as a whole in the 20s, those years that were as tough and difficult as they were formative for us all, in the construction of the revolutionary party before and after Livorno.

This heritage is not accidental, but based on a doctrine and method, coherently consistent with Marxist principles. It is a heritage that does not expect to be just defended, but must emerge again in its original entirety, and in a period of history where the theorists of the labour movement, out of party mediocrity, are championing a new social-democratic-patriotic conformism whilst claiming to be innovators in Marxism and Leninism, yet degrading the revolutionary content of socialism to a kind of despicable commodity sold by dealers in culture and politics.

These theorists who, having turned their backs on the fundamental interests of the working class, are in fact in the government of the bosses' state as a decisive force to save them from the current fatal process of disintegration and decomposition; it is no accident that this heritage of ideas and cadres is working tenaciously against the revolution, precisely when a period for its historical realisation has undeniably opened up. Thus, we have two opposing lines emerging from the current economic and political situation.

The first is the Marxist revolutionary line, which sees in the structural crisis of the capitalist system the maturation of objective conditions which are sufficient to push the proletariat, as its direct historical antagonist, to violently struggle for its total overthrow, with the aim of building a socialist society.

The second line is the pluralist one of democratic-parliamentary revisionism, already prefigured in the "historical bloc" of Gramsci, then translated and inserted — with empirical and superficial pragmatism — into the "historic compromise" of Berlinguer.[4] This aims at the economic and political restoration of the capitalist system to ensure its survival and continuity.

Introductory Note to the First Edition (1971)

A couple of lines of clarification, even if this publication, given the issues it deals with, is largely self-explanatory. Let's make it clear that we did not set out to make a comprehensive analysis of the vast and contradictory problems of Bordigism. We have merely limited ourselves to some aspects that were based on a theoretical disagreement, which focused on different problems of revolutionary politics and militancy in the party of the proletariat.

The theoretical, and sometimes harsh, controversy particularly visible in the exchange of several letters between Bordiga (Alfa) and Damen (Onorio), is not important. The names as well as the aliases, act as mere communication tools, and they are, ultimately the more or less effective and vigorous spokesmen of a reality in constant movement, which ends up by transcending the physical person who seeks to contain it within the logic of a methodology in order to interpret it better.

In any case what matters is that the disagreement acts as part of an investigation, contributes to the clarification of issues and facilitates the task proper to all research, to advance ideas and experiences. How that happens, and the price in terms of the sacrifices and rifts in human relationships, is less important.

That is why we consider that Bordiga is and remains in the history of the revolutionary movement as much for what he has given, as for what he has been unable or unwilling to give.

What he gave is the "Italian Left" which matured as the Internationalist Communist Party[5], which then took its daily struggle forward with more consistency and accuracy precisely in opposition to what Bordiga could, and should have given, but did not. Moreover, changes in human affairs, like the ceaseless change in all things are full of light and shade, affirmations and denials, so even someone political, the agitator or even the "leader", has smouldering within him unresolved contradictions without noticing or being fully aware of them.

All this constitutes the unifying fabric of this work; gathered here in well-known, and less well-known writings from the past to make them available to those who are interested as they have been out of print for a long time.

In publishing them we intend to continue the work of expanding and deepening the framework that this work has only outlined in its bare essentials. The aim? Above all else: not to break, or accept any break in the red thread of historical continuity of the "Italian Left" in its political and ideological corpus. It was the best expression of the struggles of the Italian proletariat in the Twenties, contributing to the development of a genuine class theory, not as a cultural requirement and intellectualism coaxed from books or universities, that is to say that temple of bourgeois intelligence and doctrine, as happened with the "ordinovist" experience of Gramsci, even though it developed at almost the same time as the "abstentionism" of Bordiga.

March 1971

Introductory Note to the Second Edition (1977)

In this edition, we want to complete the quite complex picture of certain aspects of the Bordiga problem, and the practical implications that stem from it. This forms a world in itself commonly called "Bordigism" which the living Bordiga would have rejected with all his Neapolitan self-assurance and which we maintain is the foundation of the "Italian Left" in an absolute unity of theory and practice up to the Congress of Lyon (1926).[6] Next we deal with how the "Left" continued to defend this class doctrine and tradition of Marxism, to which Bordiga had provided the greatest and best contribution, defending it even against Bordiga himself in many areas, whilst fighting for its very existence under the butchery of the Third International.

In a period of class reflux like this it was an issue of fundamental importance to ensure this continuity of the "Left", which was called upon to carry on with building a party as an irreplaceable instrument of revolution.

The period after Bordiga's death saw a repeat of the semi-comic drama of the struggle for the right of succession, which marked the beginning of a flowering of mostly anthological and uncritical publications made to fit the ideological-political prejudices of individuals or groups of the most diverse kinds; each has poured out as much ink as they could to adorn a wide variety of writings on Bordiga and everyone has seen and recognised for their own use and consumption a small piece of this patrimony. Are these signs of a class recovery? Is it a renewed interest in the "Left"? Or is it low level publishing speculation like the initiatives of the "gruppettari"[7] of little credit and no real political value? It is perhaps a bit of everything, but we are more inclined to believe in the latter case.

Among these publications, "Bordiga - Selected Writings" published by Franco Livorsi (Feltrinelli - 1975) is a wide-ranging collection, but it is also the most insidiously tendentious given the type of historiography on which it is based and whose obvious function, permeating every page, is pro-PCI [Italian Communist Party – translator]. But it is also obvious that it lacks the capacity to make a deeper critique of the issues it takes up. More precisely the introduction or commentary exhibits greater literary concern than any historical dimension or knowledge of the matter.

Documents of a certain political importance, for example, the letter to Karl Korsch[8] are thrown in without being properly and seriously located in their context as the historical expressions of critical developments of the ongoing political conflict, and potential state, of the contending forces in the crisis of the Communist International. The traumatic effect of the "Committee of Intesa"[9] was still in the air and the letter of Korsch gave cautious advice that was based on his harsh experience in the internal party struggles between the left and the centre that preceded the Congress of Lyon, whose consequences in terms of political and ideological deviation, grow disproportionately with the "new party" of Togliatti[10], and, even worse, with the current policy of the "historic compromise"[11] of Berlinguer.

The same applies to the letter from Bordiga to Terracini[12] which we will be criticised for calling a "last testament". Livorsi did not understand the importance of the document he had the privilege to know and make public. He has read the letters like a lover of literature and not as a specialist in history and even less as a Marxist. He should have asked a few questions and tried to formulate some answers. It is true that Marxism as a doctrine and method, does not prophesy, but offers to those that have the appropriate research tools the possibility of historical prediction. For example the explanation of the current crisis which is in the process of shaking the foundations of the most developed economy in the industrial world, is located entirely within the Marxist theory of the tendential fall of the rate of profit. This links the essential theoretical premise of Marx's "Capital" to the specific and highly original appearance of this crisis, with all its inevitable implications such as monetary turmoil, recession and, above all, inflation, phenomenon which made their first appearance, and it is no coincidence, in America, that is to say, in the technically most advanced capitalist country. This is what we, the communist left did when all other parties and groups, we repeat all, were either silent, or denied the existence of the crisis, or attributed it to super-structural contingent phenomena. But it is just historically impossible to forecast a revolutionary solution in 1975, i.e., to date to a specific year when the world revolution might break out. It would be just absurd and arbitrary science fiction.

One final note, which we hold to be particularly important, regards the attitude of Bordiga to war, and to reject the theoretical deformations by Bordiga's epigones attributed either to him, or to the communist left in general, which on this issue, as the foundation of its revolutionary strategy, has all its papers in order.

So what is the attitude that the comrades of *Programma Comunista*[13] say they have had and continue to have in the face of war? Here's how they put it:

> *"We wrote about war, for example in "The historic course of the proletarian class movement": "War is undoubtedly a result of social causes (we would say primarily economic) and its military outcomes fit as first order factors in the process of transformation of international society, interpreted from the materialist and class point*

of view." There are historical phases in which it is our duty to influence as much as we can a certain outcome of the war. In others, absolutely not. The outcome always interests us."

And, by way of illustration, they add:

"The accusation that we wanted an anti-American victory in the Korean War, does not make us either hot or cold, and only a fool can interpret it as "intellectual sympathy". We went much further: we went as far as saying it would be more advantageous for the resumption of the class struggle in the world, that America and its allies were defeated in World War II. Can it be said that we have an "intellectual sympathy" for Nazism, or just love paradox? Everyone can see the result of the Anglo-American victory: the oppression of the whole world, blurring the viewpoint of some to such an extent that they believe that it can determine everything that happens even in the remotest corner of the earth!"

Dialectics here are used with a sly purpose, dishonestly trying to deflect from their own ideological and political error in order to justify it. Whoever wrote this rubbish, picked up in a hurry in the filth of bourgeois culture, must have in his veins the social-patriotic blood that, in anticipation of the next imperialist war, already feels inclined to turn its back on the Leninist slogan of "revolutionary defeatism" by disavowing any attempt to distinguish the only strategy that puts all the protagonists of the war on the same level of responsibility, excluding none, whether the American bloc, or the Russian or Chinese bloc.

He who dares to say, "we went as far as to say it would be more advantageous for the resumption of the class struggle in the world, that America and its allies were defeated in World War II" is lying and knows it, and hasn't even the political honesty to take responsibility for what he writes by signing it. Anyway, we can demonstrate that none of the militants of our party, from its foundation to the split of 1952, (including therefore the comrades now in "Programma Comunista") ever solidarised with these positions, and never expressed opinions of this kind in written or oral statements.

It is true that there was a vague hypothesis that Bordiga formulated before or during the war, but once the war was over, he returned to his old mathematical "vice" of supposing that historical events could be understood according to the laws of probability without thinking about those future inexperienced imitators who would use it out of context thus turning a simple laboratory hypothesis, even if badly put, into a political line to be implemented.

And they add, smugly:

"Everyone can see the result of the Anglo-American victory".[14]

Would they perhaps prefer, we ask, the victory of the Italian-German axis in the context of the class struggle? Chauvinism apart, the very formulation of this hypothesis is repugnant and indicates a huge ignorance of the imperialist phenomenon which the proletariat everywhere has no choice but to try to defeat.

And now we must await the outcome of what is going on in the democratic-populist block where there is an organic inability to understand that the crisis is getting out of hand. This will hasten the re-emergence of a clearer vision of class conflict and a renewed and wider interest in problems which produced men of the intellectual stature of Bordiga, and the space for a battle of political ideas among cadres of the Italian Communist Left, which this book tries to both document and anticipate at same time.

O. D. - November 1975

The Debate with Bordiga

Amadeo Bordiga - Beyond the Myth and the Rhetoric

Our party has never made a fetish of Bordiga. Even when he was alive we openly disagreed with some of his principles, but mainly with the way his ideas were deformed by more than a few of his epigones when making use of his name. We are thus in better position to speak of him, of his great stature as a militant, of his untiring work as an organiser, but also of his own limitations.

As a result, whilst we reject the apologetic tone usually adopted in an "obituary", and which Bordiga would have rejected with his usual wisecrack that it was rubbish, we aim to show what can be accepted and defended because of its contribution to revolutionary theory, and what we don't consider to be in historic continuity with the international communist left, and particularly that which has come to be known as the "Italian Left".

What We Owe to Bordiga

We owe to Bordiga the theory of abstentionism, a tactic articulated in a period of the worst form of parliamentarism based on personal clientilism, corruption, and the jobs for the boys system that germinated in the Socialist Party in the South of Italy.   It led to the formation of the Abstentionist Fraction within the Italian Socialist Party, which created the theoretical-practical premise for the revival of marxist thought degraded by the democratic degeneration, and the profound struggle against parliament, the major bulwark of a corrupt and corrupting parliamentary democracy.

We owe to Bordiga the revival of the theoretical framework of scientific socialism, along the fundamental lines bequeathed by Marx and Engels, reinvigorating the best, the most politically aware, of the Socialist Party. This had been crushed in the vice of a social democracy which had led the Party into the seats of Montecitorio[15], which had Kautsky as its "Pope"[16] which replaced revolution with evolution, and the dictatorship of the proletariat with the dictatorship of the Giolittian[17] parliament.

We owe to Bordiga the correct theory of the relationship between party and class on which the success of revolution depends. We can state, without fear of exaggeration or contradiction, that the definition of such a relationship is a fixed point in Marxism, representing a happy fusion between the experience of the "Italian Left" and that of Lenin in the victorious conclusion to the October Revolution. And we must add that what Bordiga produced on "party and class" not only served as a Marxist reference point to the parties which were being formed in the wake of the October Revolution in the post First World War period but it is still a classic, and will remain so in the period up to the next proletarian revolutionary wave. To ignore or weaken its terms, even if done in Bordiga's name or that of some vague approximation to Bordigism, would be to undermine the meaning of the revolutionary party and its permanent role of giving a lead in working class action.

We need to go back to the Platform elaborated at the Congress of Imola[18], which posed the basis for the formation of the Communist Party of Italy at the Congress of Livorno[19](1921), to follow the formative steps of a party dynamic from which Bordiga, more and better than anyone else, drew from living experience the objective and subjective facts to elaborate his theory of the party in relation to the class.

Organic centralism? Democratic centralism? We would call it dialectical centralism, in greater coherence with the Bordiga of then, who is for us not the best Bordiga but the consistent Bordiga. Dialectical centralism because it starts with pressure from below, even if it is irrational, received and rationalised by the leadership, it returns to the rank and file to be translated into action in a concrete political way.

To give credit to a theory of organic centralism and attribute its elaboration to Bordiga who never recognised its paternity, in the name of an anti-democratic conception takes us into the realm of absurdity and makes Bordiga look ridiculous. He, on the other hand, took responsibility, and not just a formal one, for the Rome Theses[20] which in the part relating to direct and indirect tactics makes explicit the Leninist claim of accepting the opportunities offered by democracy itself in the interests of the revolutionary party.

How much importance did he give to so-called "vote counting" as a symbol of the democratic method which legitimates the existence in central committees of a majority and minority, which are mechanically linked by this vote? The writer of these lines remembers how Bordiga himself reacted to the decisions taken at the last meeting held in Naples. This had to decide whether or not to dissolve the Committee of Intesa[21] on the peremptory invitation of Zinoviev, First Secretary of the Communist International. Put in a minority, Bordiga who accepted the dissolution "sic et simpliciter" perceived with stunned sadness that it was the first time he was in a minority (the words are his own) in the very regroupment of the left which carried his name. Besides being irreverent not to say laughable is the way *Programma Comunista* puts Bordiga alongside Lenin, by praising him "as the restorer of Marxism on an even higher level, not through his personal virtues but given the historical situation he eliminated the last link with any democratic leftovers, even those which were involuntary, exterior or linguistically formal."

We have emphasised this extract in order to show their confusing remixing of ideas and methods. The Bordigist theoretical project is now up in the air, unrelated to reality in a frenzy of idealist subjectivism, a long way from serious Marxist methodology and totally alien to the work and real theoretical framework of Bordiga. We can then understand why defining and legitimising a certain organic centralism in the way the main bodies and life of the revolutionary party operate was never a preoccupation of Bordiga, nor practised by him in his life as a militant. The consequence of this theory is that, in place of a Central Committee elected in a Congress by democratic centralist methods we would have, for example, permanent Commissars who do and undo according to criteria left by the inheritance of Stalinism.

Nevertheless, it has to be recognised that it is easy to retrace in many of Bordiga's writings as in many of his personal attitudes, insights, and more or less clever and polemical original ideas, which he never followed up with any profound theoretical development through a close examination of the accumulated experience of the workers' movement at any given moment of its long history. And this is the case with "organic centralism" which some dubious Marxist epigones try to twist in a mistaken subjective way, as has already been shown in practice, thus damaging the organisation and the validity of the Leninist experience. Such damage is not always curable.

We owe to Bordiga the reversal of a political tradition of the Socialist Party where the minimum programme, that of a tactic, was everything, whilst the maximum programme, that of the strategy was nothing, reduced to a simple and ritual enunciation of a hypothetical, vague conquest of power by the working class via the law of evolution (the theory dear to reformists of the "ripe pear which falls on its own"). Like any change it had at times a paradoxical aspect where an absolute negation was replaced with an affirmation just as absolute. This was also true of Bordiga: the term "tactic" disappeared from his writings to be substituted by that of "strategy". And it gave the impression of reducing the dialectic to two fixed contradictory terms although for Bordiga it was the only, if drastic, way of really breaking the reformist tradition of political thought and practice. This put the accent on strategy which dialectically has within itself the possibility of overcoming the limited and momentary tactical issue of the present, in the fuller and more real vision of the strategic event of the future.

From personal experience we can draw on two episodes which are illuminating and particularly significant to understand how the tactical moment becomes dialectically valid within the framework of a class strategy. We are talking here of the indications indirectly given by Bordiga soon after he was thrown out of the leadership of the party of Livorno by the new Gramsci-Togliatti[22] centre regarding the line to be taken inside, and not outside, the parliamentary circus, in a situation of profound disarray provoked by the assassination of Matteotti[23]. This wasn't a moral question, he counselled, nor a question of a parliamentary secession of the Aventine type[24] following the democratic parties in the illusion that fascism could be fought in the name of a bourgeois morality offended by a vicious assassination, or in the name of the defence of parliament as the institutional guarantee of real democracy, or even in the name of the defence of the royal institutions and the prerogatives of the Savoy Monarchy.[25] This line of conduct reluctantly followed by the party centre, slowly and in zigzags, was devised and developed in Bordiga's house and echoed in the speech which Grieco read to the Chamber of Deputies, This was the same Grieco who, until then, was the chosen disciple of Amadeo and who a few months later would become the "implacable" enemy of the "Italian Left."[26]

This line was most significant for the anti-fascist tactic of the Party leadership. Faithful to the policy of the Russian state, it ended up lining up the Party on one side of an imperialist war. In its theoretical justification for this it distorted of Lenin's theory of imperialism, in a shameful and vulgar way. It so doing it undermined the activity of the revolutionary party which is to oppose imperialist war by transforming it into a class war: an ideology and task which only the communist left defended then and continues to defend today.

The second tactical experience understood as part of a strategic aim took place at the heart of the internal crisis of our party.[27] From its foundation the raison d'etre of our party, as it still is, was not to attempt a polemic addressed to the PCI from the outside to redress its ideological deviation and opportunism, but rather to establish a revolutionary party from within the "Italian Left" at a time when this was objectively missing. The disagreement mainly concerned the way of looking at the union and factory organisations which we considered to be indispensable for a revolutionary party because they not only relate to the class but the need to increase the number of cadres capable of carrying out its basic tasks which the others argued was a left social democratic practice which party policy should reject.

Bordiga, who never joined our party[28], but theoretically collaborated with it in a serious way (though not as an active militant), decided to take part in the debate. He defended the view that intermediate bodies (union organisations) are needed between the party and the class. These are the famous transmission belts without which the party would lack an instrument for directly contacting the class which the unions organise and lead in the struggle for demands – i.e. they have nothing to do with the specific tasks of the revolutionary party. But it is above all the existence of these intermediary bodies between the party and the class that creates the first and permanent condition for the party to be able to draw the working masses and their struggles towards it. Such struggles define the conditions of the party's existence, confirm the validity of its ideas, and create the possibility of its growth at the same time as that of the class as a whole. Through them the party can prepare its political instruments and human material in order to join in the daily struggle and thus increase and deepen it in order to raise the particular and immediate to the universal. In other words, widening and deepening the objective and super-structural possibilities for revolutionary growth.

This intervention had a small echo at the time amongst those comrades who were disgusted by union activity with the real animosity of neophytes: but once the split had taken place in the internationalist organisation the U-turn which we all know about then took place without any critical justification which a change of position of this type would normally merit.

It's worth recounting these two episodes to show how carefully Bordiga, and with him the "Italian Left", confronted and resolved the difficult problem of revolutionary tactics both in the realm of theory and in its practical application in order to expose the myth, if it was needed, of a Bordiga, and a left wing of the Party, incapable of grappling with tactical problems. What is true about this accusation, so dear to Gramsci and Togliatti at the time of their tireless and dark attacks on the leadership of the Communist Party of Italy (in 1923) to have the left replaced (a substitution which took place it is worth repeating, not through a decision of the party membership which was overwhelmingly on the left[29], but by virtue of the new Russian policy to which the Centre of the Third International conformed in every aspect, even meddling in the internal activities of the parties of the single sections of the International), is that the Left has always, openly and resolutely opposed tactics as such. In other words tactics which are detached from any class strategy: the Left openly and resolutely opposed the short-term, immediate tactics of Gramsci and Togliatti which made the Communist Party of Italy the party of systematic compromise, as well as pursuing the useless policy[30] of an Italian, peaceful path to socialism.

Up to now we have briefly examined in an objective way what Bordiga, the militant revolutionary, passed on in the way of a body of thought and lessons. These were born out of an experience which covered a period of struggle which was one of the most intense in the revolutionary movement. This experience undoubtedly shaped the inheritance of the Italian Left and therefore the revolutionary party. We would however be in dereliction of our duty as militants of a revolutionary party if we were not also objective in analysing the limits of his thought and personality. We cannot remain silent, for sentimental or supposed politically opportunist reasons, on what in the work and attitude of our comrade we consider contradictory and a deviation from our tradition.

Bordiga's Limitations

Bordiga lacked a true evaluation of the dialectic because his education was largely based on scientific facts[31] which led him to see the world and life on the level of rational development when the reality of social existence and of revolutionary struggle often put it in a world which was largely shaped by irrational impulses. The methodology based on mathematical certainties, which belongs to science, is not always in agreement with a methodology based on the dialectic which is movement and contradiction and this is no small matter when it comes to the analysis and perspectives of revolutionary politics. It is in the light of this underestimation of the dialectical method in the Marxist sense that we identify the reasons for the futility of the Bologna Congress (1919) in terms of achieving a fundamental clarity about reality and the immediate perspectives for the Socialist Party. It was practically finished as a party of revolution, though alive and kicking as a parliamentary party, and there was a need to work in that Congress for the formation of a new party, either through a split by those who were in favour of revolutionary action, or by the coming together of the revolutionary left inside the old structure to wait for the right moment to make the break. This was both a necessary and sufficient condition to bring into being an ideologically and organisationally mature communist party which could take on the role of spur and guide to the working class whilst a revolutionary outcome was still possible. At Livorno (1921) the situation had already changed and the forces of the working class were in fact in retreat under the pressure of the Fascist reaction. Bordiga himself, who took on the major responsibility for the theoretical and political orientation of the abstentionist left, didn't understand that at Bologna, and not later, a start should have been made in building the Communist Party. Such a historic endeavour demanded a platform which should not have had a tactical expedient like abstentionism as its essential component but a platform, not unlike that of Lenin's party, which attracted around it all the forces of the left ready to fight for the proletarian revolution. In such a party abstentionism would have been able to play a significant role, (even if not pre-eminent one), in acting as a healthy antidote to the rapidly growing electoralism of the worst type.

A correct dialectical interpretation does not pose the question in terms of fundamental contradictions as in the case in point, electoralism and abstentionism but in terms of the historical motives of a class in its economic and political totality. The proletariat, the subject, is the class opposed to those who rule it, the bourgeoisie (capitalists).

This period of Bordiga's personal and political life practically ended with the ejection of the Left from the leading bodies of the Party and as a result the compulsory end of Bordiga's leadership. But above all it was the consciousness of the collapse of the Third International as the centre of leadership of the world revolution which brought about in Bordiga that psycho-political trauma which accompanied him for more than forty years until his death[32]: an inferiority complex which prevented him from putting out of his mind the butchery of that enormous international organisation which collapsed so suddenly on top of those who had believed in its continuity and force with a certainty which had more of the mystical than the scientific.

His political behaviour, his constant refusal to take on a politically responsible attitude, has to be considered in this particular climate. Thus many political events, some of great historic importance, such as the Trotsky-Stalin conflict and Stalinism itself were disdainfully ignored without an echo. The same was true for our Fraction abroad in France and Belgium, the ideology and the politics of the party of Livorno, the Second World War and finally the alignment of the USSR with the imperialist front. Not a word, not a line on Bordiga's part appeared throughout this historic period which was on a wider and more complex level than the First World War. By contrast the First World War had offered to Lenin the objective basis for a Marxist analysis condensed into "Imperialism as the Highest Stage of Capitalism" and the "State and Revolution" pillars of the revolutionary doctrine and theoretical premises of the October Revolution.

We had to wait for the end of the war and the Fascist experience to re-establish real contact with the comrades and members of the organisation who still remained. First of all there was contact with Bordiga to let us know what he was thinking on the major issues and what he intended to do as a communist militant. It wasn't a case of asking Bordiga to assume responsibility at the centre of the Party even if his support as advisor and "anonymous" collaborator of the Party was full and constant when he was not being inspired by a general political orientation which was not always in tune with that of the Party.

His way of speaking diverged from ours even if his method of analysis was more or less as always. He maintained that we should not speak of the Russian economy in terms of "state capitalism" but of "state industrialism", not of a socialist October Revolution but of an anti-feudal revolution and, therefore, of an economy which was tending towards capitalism. But he did not seem greatly convinced of what he was saying and the corrections he brought into his thinking a short time later seem to confirm this. And then what is the reason for an ideological cover so fragile and in so obvious contradiction with his past and above all with the points of the platform of the "Italian Left" which were developed by Bordiga himself? We don't want to get involved in a psycho-political drama where the main component is fear, even and above all, physical, of a rupture with the past which he had built with his consciousness, even more with his intelligence and creativity, the masterpiece of his political life lived so intensely in the 1920s. The label "state capitalism" had a class significance, "state industrialism" did not. He thus left things as they had been or as he wanted them to be.

This is why we think it is a positive thing to return now to these debates with a more mature and perceptive experience than we could have had in the 1940s or so. A late and not very convincing justification of the theory of "state industrialism" re-appeared almost incidentally in *Programma Comunista* No. 3 (February 1966) from the same author. We copy from the article "The New Enterprise Statute in Russia"

"First remark: the statement that state enterprises are "principal links" implies the existence of non-state enterprises and as a result "private" activity in the vulgar sense of the term and reconfirms our old assumption against "state capitalism" in Russia in which we recognised rather a "state industrialism". Other "links" exist, other firms, in the Russian economy which compete in the economic process."

The justification which the author himself gives for it not only confirms our analysis at the time but clearly demonstrates the fact that his imprecision in relation to the nature of the soviet economy was essential to him. It was useful then for hiding the political desire to reject (we say "then" because that's where the evidence comes from) any rigid class formulation like "state capitalism" and to which all the theoretical and political framework of the Internationalist Communist Party had been linked since it was founded.

The theoretical justification he gives us borders on the limits of banality if by this he aimed to create a new economic category which had never existed before, either in the history of the capitalist economy, or in the experience of the first phase of the socialist state.

This phase of development of the capitalist economy was clearly outlined by Engels in his masterly "Anti-Duhring"

> "...the transformation of the great establishments for production and distribution into joint-stock companies [trusts] and state property show how unnecessary the bourgeoisie are for that purpose. All the social functions of the capitalist are now performed by salaried employees." op. cit. p. 385 (Moscow 1954)

This is not a quibble over words but a political judgement of fundamental importance if there is a will to take the revolutionary party down a clear and coherent path in the face of the most disconcerting problems in the post-war world. The statement that the state enterprises act as principal links in the national economy implies the existence of non-state enterprises, and consequently "private" activity, which is characteristic of the entire unequal development of capitalism right up to its period of maximum development. It also belongs to the lower phase of socialism which increases the power of "its" state capitalism and overcomes it in the dialectical form of the socialist state gradually getting rid of capitalist and pre-capitalist relics in the state enterprises which the revolution has inevitably dragged behind it in the historic course of building a socialist society.

And it is this type of state capitalism which Lenin conceived and which the later strengthening of the socialist sector would have to overcome and win over within the framework of a revolutionary power where the greatest guarantee was the exercise of the political dictatorship of the armed proletariat. But the nature of the state capitalism which the revolutionary party was faced with in the midst of the Second World War and in the immediate post-war period (this is what happened at the centre of our organisation and to which this note refers) was radically different and had very different characteristics which we would like to quickly examine even if compelled to be brief:

State capitalism under Stalin did not tend toward socialism but towards the consolidation of the power of traditional capitalism in the form of strongly centralised state enterprises, made possible by the passage of the private industrial economy into the orbit of the state set up by the October Revolution.

The insertion of the USSR in the Second World War had no element of socialist justification, but on the other hand thousands of a bourgeois justifications of a capitalist nature, with obvious imperialist implications, as the Yalta Conference between Stalin, Roosevelt and Churchill (1945) would later show. This placed Russia amongst the great beneficiaries in the share-out of war booty. It is the same unscrupulous tactical elasticity which saw Russia at first connive with Hitler (as if with Hitler's battalions you could get to socialism) in the partition of Poland and then after a 180 degree turn alongside the Western democracies (as if socialism could be a common goal of the greatest plutocracies in the world).

The Soviet economy remained, in its fundamental structure as it was in Stalin's time. Khruschev's liberalisation, more theory than reality, and the anti-demagogic nature of the technocrats[33] taken together, have not done much to bring significant changes, or only in just a few sectors. They do however reveal interesting episodes in a series of super-structural crises in the political, economic and military apparatuses, as the experience of the last few decades abundantly demonstrate.

We need to make a clear class distinction between the time which could be defined as that of Lenin and that which began with Stalin, and which has continued without deep or substantial modifications by his successors.

The time of Lenin, from the October Revolution to the start of the New Economic Policy (NEP) is characterised by the workers' state based on the Soviets and the Communist Party and all based on the armed forces of the working class. The working class exercised its own dictatorship even though facing obstacles and difficulties of every kind. These were provoked by the temporary halt to the offensive of the forces of the international proletariat and the immediate prospect of a concrete revolutionary extension across Europe. In order to stay on course towards socialist objectives the dictatorship made concessions to the class enemy as an indispensable short term tactic within the strategic vision of returning to the revolutionary offensive. In the big picture of Lenin's time state capitalism represents a calculated risk of a sought after and temporary break from the objective needs of the market economy, which though restricted was fraught with danger. The market was controlled by the state of the dictatorship in which the game of supply and demand, the function of capital, profit itself, and the use of surplus value were marginal features, regulated in the general interests of the socialist economy itself.

These fundamentally important reasons, acquired by the revolutionary vanguard since the beginning of the process of degeneration, have been the basis of its struggle. This was originally articulated through open denunciation, then through its organisational and political separation, first in the work of the left fraction[34] then in the party.[35] In the process of defining itself as a party it rediscovered the basis of revolutionary communism and internationalism.

We are not concealing the fact that within these problems which we have raised a line of political coherence emerged and developed which must appear for what it is. It cannot be silenced nor be distorted by the arbitrary superimpositions of a mystificatory character on it.

And this has been, and still is, our finest, even if most thankless, battle. To each his own and we need to recognise in Bordiga a logical coherence in his attitude which began with his silent obstructionism in the Central Committee[36] after the Lyons Congress (1926)[37], and found its natural conclusion in the letter/testament addressed, it was no accident, to Terracini.[38]

This discussion of ours may seem, on a sentimental level, bitter and perhaps inhuman, but we are referring here to the value Marxists give to the role of human beings in the ups and downs of history and we are sure we have interpreted the profound meaning of the teachings of Bordiga himself. He wanted the interests of revolutionary action to be above any political-ideological by-product, and that also includes degenerated Bordigism.

Onorato Damen

Five Letters and an Outline of the Disagreement

The letters which follow with their "Foreword" were published in *Prometeo* (No 3 April 1952) soon after the split in the Internationalist Communist Party. Onorio is the pseudonym of Onorato Damen, Alfa is Bordiga.

Foreword

You cannot eliminate one basic assumption, one substantial part of this philosophy of Marxism (it is as if it were a block of steel) without abandoning objective truth, without falling into the arms of bourgeois-reactionary falsehood.
Lenin *Marxism and Empirio-criticism* (this English version taken from his *Collected Works* Volume XIII (1927-8 edition, Lawrence and Wishart)

We have reached a point in the discussion of disagreements in our organisation as a result of the different way of considering, from a Marxist standpoint, some problems inherent in the present period of the capitalist crisis. The publication of these five letters, which have the merit of initiating this indispensable theoretical clarification, has thus never been more necessary nor more opportune.

The polite polemical encounter by letter between Alfa and Onorio rather than between x and y has no special value; what is important in these circumstances is the theoretical concern which animates it, the conviction of the contending parties to feel themselves equally faithful in interpreting the same doctrine.

What is certain however is that by publishing these writings we are not revealing any secret correspondence. We are not attempting some speculative polemic but start from the conviction, a conviction which is not ours alone. This is that when a revolutionary thinks and writes to explain to himself, to interpret and understand more deeply the problems of the revolutionary struggle, it ceases to be a personal activity and becomes the common patrimony of the class to which he belongs.

It is absurd to think that what one of us writes and maintains in private on these subjects should only be thought of as valuable and important from this point of view, and this ends if it is revealed and submitted to the outside, collective, critique of the party. This is especially so when these statements and theoretical elaborations relate to problems of strategy and tactics linked to the revolutionary party's very reason for existence, both in the present and the very near future.

From reading these letters it appears clear that the basis of dissent lies, as ever, in a different evaluation of the Marxist dialectic, a different way of adhering to this doctrine. In reality differences of interpretation of historical materialism are as old as Marxism itself and it seems almost as if this disagreement gets new vitality with the appearance of every new generation of revolutionaries.

Is there a danger today that our party will be uprooted from its class terrain, from its ideology and its historic tasks through a false application of revolutionary theory? We reply without hesitation; yes, because it is only today that the extent and depth of the bourgeois world crisis that puts to the test the ideologies, the political programmes, the parties and the individual combatants, and which reveal in their true light both the correct and the weak aspects of any body of doctrine and any theoretical formulation. Under the pressure of events and their very coherence that which seemed secondary, marginal, redundant, and could be ignored and seen as a purely personal state of mind, intellectual arrogance, at the same time paradoxically inoffensive and agreeable, is now pushed to the surface, clarified, almost makes itself a material force and is dialectically forced to show what it is, and what it's critique is worth.

The proletarian party now makes this theoretical contribution its own and assimilates it, now rejects it as alien to its class nature, by refracting it through the prism of action. It continually compares any theory with past experience and the interest it can draw on, on condition that it is not just a fleeting and circumstantial idea and that it does not contradict its ultimate aims.

Overturning Praxis

Let's examine Alfa's schema[39] which express his way of conceiving the dialectic. *Descending curve or branch of an ascending curve?* The first formulation is unacceptable if we attribute to it a gradualism which excludes "shocks, shakes, somersaults", the second "the branch of an ever ascending curve" is unacceptable if in this real world of economic things there is also no corresponding link to the rise or increased power of the contradictions which at the same time also have a tendency "to decline". In this case capitalism would be moribund for those of us who have learned from Lenin:

> On the whole, capitalism is growing far more rapidly than before; but this growth is not only becoming more and more uneven in general, its unevenness also manifests itself, in particular, in the decay of the countries which are richest in capital (Britain). Imperialism, the Highest Stage of Capitalism (From Lenin *Selected Works* Moscow 1977 p. 728)

Bordiga's graph expressing the "the branches of the ascending curves" does not indicate in any way the dialectical contradiction in which

> It is through its very progress that capital doubly prepares its final collapse… the economic progress of capital as it gets bigger bit by bit aggravates class antagonisms and economic and political anarchy throughout the world to the point where it provokes the revolt of the international proletariat against its dominion a long time before its

economic evolution would have reached its final consequence: the absolute and exclusive
power of capitalist production in the world.
Rosa Luxemburg

It is true that imperialism hugely increases and provides the means for prolonging the life of capital but at the same time it constitutes the surest means for cutting it short. This schema of the ever-ascending curve not only does not show this but in a certain sense denies it. It is on this false interpretation of the dialectical problem that the theory of the uselessness of creating a party in a counter-revolutionary period such as the present is based. It is a theory which diminishes the party, in its structure, its tasks and its action, when others have already built it. It limits the function of its press to a mere theoretical catalogue which mechanically repeats the past without shedding any light on why a revolutionary vanguard, solidly anchored in the life of the problems of the proletariat, and their transformation onto the level of the historic continuity of the revolutionary struggle, is needed.

Starting from this understanding of revolutionary doctrine we arrive at the most recent novelty … the dialectic of accepting a minimum of interest in practical action if it is justified by an adequate quantitative return, such as, for example, participation of the party in the electoral struggle would still be possible in spite of one's abstentionist convictions, if the objective means for a decent quantitative result existed. In relation to this Alfa's games and somersaults over abstentionist theory are significant. He insisted on the most rigid abstentionism before, and right up to, the Congress of Imola in the course of which he agreed to abandon *"abtorto collo"* [against his will] this single well-known characteristic of the Neapolitain opposition; at Livorno he accepted elections *tout court* [without a quibble] until the Rome Congress; he returned to abstentionism when the political forces of the Party were in fact dispersed and with them the leadership of the Left of the Party, and today he is an abstentionist *maybe yes, maybe no* and for elections *maybe yes, maybe no* when he considers participation once again, if as a preliminary the certainty of numerical success were guaranteed.

Still within the framework of this interpretation … of Marxism according to Bordiga;

> *the analysis which claims that all the conditions for revolution exist but what is missing is a revolutionary leadership makes no sense. It is correct to say that the organ of leadership is indispensable but its appearance depends on the general conditions of struggle themselves, never on the genius or value of a leader or a vanguard.*

This reasoning would be the fundamental argument to show the theoretical validity of his schema relative to the overturning of praxis for which *just as determinism excludes for the individual the possibility of will or consciousness, the necessary conditions for action, the overturning of praxis uniquely allows them into the Party as a result of its general historical elaboration.*

In this schema a mathematical logic prevails to the detriment of common sense, a determinism of "things" unconnected to the activity of human beings for whom it is mathematically certain that if a revolutionary leadership has defects on the political scene it is because the revolutionary conditions are not there; and vice versa, if the revolutionary conditions really exist then there will be no lack of revolutionary leadership. Put like this the dialectic of Marx is on the same level as ... the official policy of the Catholic Church which takes its evangelical creed from the preaching of Christ.

Let's make our thinking on this more precise. The terms of the schema in question have to be "historicised" in the sense that in the determinist "prius" [i.e. what has gone before] there are not only in play individual impulses produced by economic stumuli and appetites but that these stimuli and appetites have to be understood in the sense of the shifts and changes in the total process of the capitalist economy, in the level of development of the means of production, in their technical sophistication, in variations of the market, in its recurrent crises, in the growing domination of financial capital, etc. etc.

The formation and modification of human consciousness, its transformation into will and action, are reflections at the level of social and political life of what is produced in the sub-soil of the economy but between the determining factors and a world determined by the superstructure there is a relationship which in its turn reacts on the base as an indispensable element in completing any historical event. No geometric scheme or arithmetic calculation can encapsulate this relationship between the world which determines and that which is determined. There is no eternally true and valid formula which says that this impulse comes from the subsoil of the economy or from what is happening in the superstructure.

In our case an adequate and timely crystallisation of revolutionary consciousness and the will to act does not always correspond to the objective conditions offered by the capitalist crisis. The first post-war crisis (1919) in Germany and Italy tragically showed us a proletariat instinctively brought to understand the need for a struggle for power but which lacked a revolutionary leadership. The history of workers' struggles is full of examples of favourable situations in which the proletariat missed the bus due to the presence of a Party not up to the task of leadership.

This is the focal point not only for interpreting the dialectic but also for the nature and function of the class party. The birth of the party does not depend, and on this we agree, *"on the genius or value of a leader or a vanguard"* but it is the historic existence of the proletariat as a class which poses, not merely episodically in time and space the need for the existence of its Party. The proletariat would reduce itself to being mere plebians if it lost its class character as the antagonist of capitalism; and its possibility as an exploited class which struggles for its own defence and liberation would be thwarted and rendered null and void if the motivation and physical forces for a revolutionary leadership were not produced from within it through its own struggles.

But what, in reality, are the relations between party and class? We have to fight as foreign to Marxism the schema which rejects the existence of the Party in the period of counter-revolution and which is confined to a restricted vanguard reduced to the melancholy task of study; which foresees the appearance of the Party in the fire of the revolutionary assault and gives to the Party, and only to it, the function of subject in the overturning of praxis. We don't know, for how long and through what magical virtue, the body (constituted by the class) should remain without a head (the class Party).

In this schema, given the erroneous conception of the nature and function of the Party a totally catastrophic idea is precisely defined with the sudden appearance of the Party in the final period of the crisis of capitalism, leaping who knows how, from the head of Jove to resolve alone the miracle of overturning praxis. In this conception the Party is detached from the class and its genetic development as a whole, this Party to which individual workers and the labouring class stimulate through their consciousness and will, an accumulation of the necessary revolutionary potential without which the return to the determining base would not be possible in the same way that a revolutionary outcome for a class detached from its Party would not be possible.

All this breaks the dialectical process that Marxism historically attributes to the class as the historic antithesis of the bourgeoisie; class antithesis not Party antithesis because the contradictions are class against class and not party against party because at the end the subversive force is the class and not the Party. The Party makes revolutionary activity more perceptible and gives it real force, it renders it more conscious, and points the way towards it. In this sense the Party is a Party of the class, in the class, not outside the class, and distinct from it. The dialectical overthrow is carried out by the class as a whole, and not by the Party in place of the class: except that there will be no shift from the class in itself towards the class for itself where the nerve centre preparing and leading it (i.e. the Party) is absent.

Nothing takes place automatically independently of human action. There exists no development of the superstructure (moral, juridical, philosophical, literary, artistic etc) which does not rest on economic development. *"But all these react upon one another and also upon the economic base."* Engels *Letter of 1894*

Thus the question of the *"returning influence"* of the superstructure on the economic base and on the productive forces of society is made more precise with the statement that *"amongst the different series of social phenomenon there is an unending process of reciprocal action"*, cause and effect substitute themselves one for the other. The *"theory of reciprocal action"* was made clear and summed up in masterly fashion by Engels:

> *"People make their history themselves, only in given surroundings which condition it and [in einem gegebenen, sie bedingenden Milieu] on the basis of actual relations already existing, among which the economic relations, however much they may be influenced by the other political and ideological ones, are still ultimately the decisive ones, forming the red thread which runs through them and alone leads to understanding." [Letter of 1894]*

Where these two interpretations of historical materialism and the dialectical method diverge is inevitably the starting point for different ways of understanding the role of the party, of evaluating its immediate and long-term tasks and therefore of conceiving and carrying out its tactics and strategy.

Those who have the responsibility to lead the revolutionary party and who, when we examine the problems, start from an interpretation based on an mechanical economism, you can be sure, will always remain waiting for the revolution until it is knocking on the door to warn us that the time has arrived to build the class party and proceed to the insurrection.

The theory which leads to the affirmation that there is nothing for the party to do in this period of counter-revolution is absolutely unacceptable, and which in a formally logical coherence is of the view that is it useless and damaging to proceed to the formation of the party or keep it going and this until the point where we no longer find ourselves faced with a radical reversal of the present relations of force between the two historic classes.

Faced with the present problems of imperialism and war the formal coherence of this arbitrary and mistaken interpretation of Marxism is also a departure from the fundamental line of class analysis and revolutionary interests if it ends up desiring the victory of bourgeois forces which carry within them the future of capitalist progress. To flirt or have flirted with forms of dictatorship just to cock a snook at democratic forms pretends to ignore or forget that Lenin, with the small dispersed nuclei of the Bolshevik Party, insisted, right in the middle of the war and after the terrible collapse of the Second International, on the possibility, even in physical terms, of a revolutionary revival and victory.

Faced with the alternative of remaining what we have always been, or bending to an attitude of platonic and intellectualist aversion to American capitalism, and benevolent neutrality towards Russian capitalism only because it is not yet capitalistically mature, we don't hesitate to restate the classical position which internationalist communists take on all the protagonists in the second imperialist conflict, which is not to hope for a victory of one or other of the adversaries, but to seek a revolutionary solution to the capitalist crisis.

Faced with the alternative of saving the Party at all cost or accepting a leadership of men with ideas and methods which would oblige us, in the face of a third world war, to go back to a position of political nihilism, to abandon our place in the struggle and liquidate every form of organisation, as happened on the eve of the Second World War, we have no hesitation in reacting to this renewed underhand effort and to defend the party in the role which proletarian interests and revolutionary struggle have assigned to it.

This is what has led, and had to lead, to a theoretical conflict which we wanted to clarify here, even in the doctrinal domain. As such however, this is not simply a theoretical question but also means a political divergence over strategy and tactics which are no longer aiming for the same class objective along the line of the proletarian revolution.

[First Letter] Onorio to Alfa 6 July 1951

I have examined your edited document tracing your reasons for attacking certain theoretical and political positions prevailing in some international groups almost all coming from Trotskyism, and I'll say straight away that, in some ways, I preferred your oral exposition in Rome to the written version, for its greater acuteness of analysis and perhaps also for its greater completeness.

I'll summarise some of my hurried observations for you.

In section 5 of your basic lines of orientation you state that in Russia the economy tends to capitalism and give the reason for it on page 8 where you write that

> *"The monetary, mercantile, income and ownership character of the predominant Russian economic fabric is not nullified by the statification of the big industries, services, etc."*

It looks to me as if you are not making clear here the idea of a soviet economy as a state capitalist structure in a world economy which has reached its highest stage of monopoly.
The tendency to an ever greater intervention of the state, which is characteristic in this economic period of the most highly industrialised countries, finds in the soviet economy it's most complete, defined and organic expression. Being in the general line of development of monopoly capitalism enabled Russia to miss out more than one stage, thanks to the October Revolution which allowed the most absolute centralisation of the economy within the orbit of the state. In addition, thanks to the Stalinist counter-revolution, it made use of this enormous centralised economic potential to massively increase the power of the state and open the way to this latest capitalist experience.

The protagonist of this historic period is therefore the state whose economy reproduces, on a wider scale perhaps, the methods and characteristics which really belong to capitalist production and distribution (wage labour, market, surplus value, accumulation etc...).

What is the new class which exercises its dictatorship through the means of this state? The enormous power of the soviet state cannot have failed to concretely resolve the problem of a homogenous and strong ruling class through the consciousness which it has of its own being and of the historic function which it is called upon to carry out. Further in section 5 of the basic lines of orientation on the

> *"conveyance of class forces in every country to the terrain of autonomy in the face of all the states"*

You entrust the supreme task to

"Breaking capitalist power in the more advanced industrialised countries of the West who block the road to revolution".

Which leads us to ask: is it only the most advanced industrialised economies of the West which stand in the way of revolution?

Further on, on page 3 still in the same argument you write

"This confused and unfavourable outcome for the proletarian struggle at the same time as the unstoppable increase in highly concentrated capitalist industrialisation, both in its intensity in the countries where it started, as well as in its wider extension throughout the inhabited world, is to the advantage of the advanced countries through which the greatest force in modern imperialism, the American, tends, according to the nature and needs of any great concentration of metropolitan capital, of productive forces, of power, brutally smashing all territorial and social obstacles, to subject the masses of the entire world to its exploitation and oppression."

We have to again ask ourselves: is it really only America, the greatest force of modern imperialism, which tends to subjugate, etc. the masses of the entire world?

In another step in another of your recent writings, which I don't however have to hand, you speak of a peaceful Russia in the face of a bellicose America.

"The leitmotif is therefore always the same: only through an error of soviet diplomacy or through a mistaken calculation by its politicians such as that in the last war with a political strategy – allowing the remnants of the great Communist International to be shamefully dissolved – (wasn't it already rotten to the bone and tied body and soul to imperialism?) which led to the reinforcement of western imperialist power which the Russian government and state recognised too late as a greater threat than Germany to their now openly national interests."

In short Moscow is seen as the centre of a mistaken, ineffectual policy, even from the point of view of pure national interests, and not as the centre of imperialism on a par with the USA with a Russian perspective for world domination.

The proletariat's anti-capitalist revolution will not leave out, we would like to think, the soviet regime, and *it does not move according to some order of priority of capitalist countries to be overthrown, but strikes at the adversary when and how it can,* wherever it appears the weakest. In 1917 for example it struck international capitalism in Tsarist Russia which was certainly not considered ripe for socialism compared to Britain or Germany etc and we know very well why.

For the rest, I would stress the critical analysis which allows us to state the following: that the aversion to Stalinism of all the splits started more from an impulse to defend the individual, and national independence, rather than from the needs of the class and the concern to bring living and active material to the reconstruction of the international party of the proletariat.

[Second Letter] Alfa to Onorio 9 July 1951

I certainly appreciated the contribution of your observations to the international appeal proposed by me and I am responding immediately on the principal issues.

I take first your observation relating to page 3. You ask: Is it only America that tends to subject others, etc? – but you yourself have quoted my qualification: according to the nature and necessity of the greatest metropolitan concentration of capital, of forces of production and of power.

Therefore, not just America, but *any* concentration. Where, and what, do you find in the different historic stages of these concentrations? This is the point. We have to take into account: its territory and its resources, population, development of its industrial machinery, numbers of modern proletarians, colonial possessions as well as raw materials, human reserves, markets, historic continuity of its state power, outcome of the recent wars, progress in the global concentration of forces both in production and in armaments. And then we can conclude that in 1905 six great powers were on the same level or almost, in 1914 it was only Germany and England which competed against each other: today? If we examine all those factors we can see that America is the No. 1 concentration in the sense that, (way beyond the rest and it is beyond doubt that in any future conflict it will win) it can certainly intervene anywhere where an anti-capitalist revolution is victorious. In this historic sense I say that today the revolution, which can only be international, will waste its time if it does not take out the US state in Washington D.C.[40] Does this mean that we are a long way from that? Okay.

We come then to the usual question: the analysis and definition of Russian society today. You know full well that I think that on this point one can and must say as little as possible, and that with circumspection. It is an elaboration carried out by the movement over a long period, it is a new given in history, the first example of a revolution which shrivels and disappears. I will give what contribution I can but I don't believe in the existence of some high priest who can reply by opening the Talmud and pointing to this or that verse. Naturally I said more about this in Rome and will say more about it in *Prometeo* in good time. You compare two things which are on different levels: in truth I am somewhat worried by such lack of understanding amongst all, truly all, I am not making a personal argument, who feel driven and predisposed to take on the task of leadership. The appeal has some value in a negative sense (like all the decisive propositions of Marxism which if not really negative are at least "alternative") it is useful, in establishing demarcations between us and others you like to call "political" since that is an adjective you like. You can read in a few minutes that over several hours in Rome we dealt with problems which were on one side scientific analysis (I would say "research", "examinations" as I am not keen on "analysis" even if it is fashionable) and on the other of tactical praxis. Both together, for greater force, completeness and detail.

I now come to Russia. I would like those who collaborate in defining the appeal to formulate positively the alternatives which they are proposing. Does the formula of the monopolistic and state capitalist phase appear complete to you? It is extremely undecided for me. You are applying it to the regime of Mussolini as well as to present day Britain and to Russia. Two different ways to arrive at similar positions? To be sure it is a good propaganda concept but for pity's sake let's avoid confusions. In what I say don't think I am identifying in what you have written the mistakes I am going to indicate, but you must precisely propose your version of the argument; you and any of the others who have made observations, work which I believe will be useful in that it is very different from the "material for the whole organisation", with its usual this or that is stupid.

It is not accurate to say that the bourgeoisie was the protagonist in one period of capitalism and that the State is the protagonist today. Class and State are different things and ideas are not interchangeable. Before you still had the State, and after you still have the Class. The State is not the leading factor in economic facts but is derived from them: if politics don't arise from the economy but the economy from politics and the management of power then the Marxist interpretation of history is dead (and those who think that should say it clearly!) and the old theories, which still seem new to imbeciles, that history is created from the desires of the leaders, and the need of those who have wealth to rule, are back in fashion.

The same stupidity is more or less arrived at by those who ask: in the first phase the protagonists in the duel were the bourgeoisie and proletariat, now let's take a torch and go in search of the third ... man. A third class? They won't find it and so the response is: the State, just as those who were searching for the third man would say: here he is, it is this pair of trousers. Or rather the response is that the bureaucracy is the new class. What the devil does this mean? I don't know if you have my writings on this: all class regimes have had a bureaucracy: it cannot be "a class". In our language the bureaucracy is one of the "forms of production" whilst the classes are forces of production, throughout history.

You will know among my texts (it would be useful if you would criticise them and raise objections) those in which it says that state capitalism doesn't mean the subjection of capital to the state but a further subjection of the state to capital.

Capital – capitalism – capitalist or bourgeois class – capitalist or bourgeois state. We are not mixing things up. We need historic order to make some sense in our heads.

Formerly there was already capital but not yet the rest. This capital began to concentrate forces of production (materials, men, machines) and capitalism started but the State was not yet bourgeois. Then came the bourgeois class, the union of all those who were high up in the new capitalist system of production but were low in the State. This class took power because capitalism needed very different *forms* from the old ones. We had a new State, with a new bureaucracy, and so on.

Marx (take him or leave him) pointed out that in "post-capitalism" (another stupid fashionable word): the proletariat takes power and ushers in socialism. The bourgeoisie and the bourgeois state oppose it.

What precisely is the class? A collection of people? That's a bad way to put it. It is instead a "network of interests". You don't like my complicated formula of a meeting of interests? I see it as a wise step forward whilst I see little in the confused play on words: capital, State, bureaucracy.

When classes were still castes, and then orders, it coincided with fixed groups of people (of families). After the bourgeois revolution, despite the cardinal right of inheritance it was no longer so. A peer of France was a nobody across the Channel. A capitalist is a someone everywhere.

All these elementary things – which I don't spell out as an adversary – it is just better to repeat them as you are being difficult – open up in the Russian question. Admittedly we don't have enough facts (Marx could call on all the material in the British Museum, faithful picture of English capitalism, but we cannot set up in Moscow where we would find only fake documents) on the official definition of the dominant class in Russia. We cannot make a single step forward without the famous "bureaucracy". I have already done a lot in recognising the existence of a strata of *entrepreneurs* without property titles to the means of production who benefit in an important way from profits. But the bureaucracy can also be like that in our countries, an instrument of the latter and their big businesses, like a business agent abroad.

The bureaucracy governs and gorges itself for itself alone? But what can this mean? The State personalised in a network of functionaries, the class –State? Nonsense.

To us, it is *Monsieur de la Palisse*.[41] In state capitalism there are only bureaucrats in the population, even factory workers are functionaries. The Boss-State, an old anarchoid formula. However this is a text that I intend to write and this is not the place to say more on the Russian economic argument.
But you say to me, why are your guns just trained on the West? Anyone would think that the revolution need not take place in Russia. I accept the comment: I am going

to say something to avoid this great misunderstanding. Though it is difficult to give the laws of the process for a failed revolution we can say that any further process can be nothing but a new class revolution.

I have never said or written otherwise. But we will also give here, though badly and in a great hurry and *ad usum Onorii*[42], not "for all the organisation", a little clarification. You are right that the texts must be done. It is better to do them than to argue.

Neither you nor I have the keys and levers to unleash the revolution in Washington or in Moscow and we cannot decide just what turn history will take. The revolution can begin anywhere, as in 1917. Fine. But was it an act of will or a product of history? What were the circumstances? Feudal regime, military defeat, split between the State and the bourgeois class etc, this is well known. And then we say "the *world* revolution can begin anywhere".

Be careful that you too could be a Staliniser. It is Stalin who says the Russian proletarian revolution was born, grew and will live there on its own.

The question has therefore to be seen internationally. Just as with the economy, "this network of interests" which is the bourgeois regime, is international. So also in politics, the question of power is international. In the both senses these characteristics have gone on being clarified for a century.

Today the historical issue is this: the Stalinists put all their propaganda into attacking America, and on peace. The proletariat follows them and up to now that has been undeniable. You recognise, or at least concede, that it is important to make clear the danger of opposing them through liberalism, of persons or peoples, and not on a class basis.

We are talking about not just limiting ourselves to accusing Stalinism over its Russian nationalist errors but of basing ourselves on the anti-class nature of its position: 1944 all its forces with America, dissolution [of the Comintern in 1943 – translator] etc – 1951, all against America, in order to say you betrayed us then, and, as you rightly say, a long time before that.

It is already very daring (in the struggle against the terrible competition of misinformation in which the West and East compete) to "politically" say to the Stalinists: take care, you won't beat America this way, we the defenders of the class will beat it, it can only be beaten by the world proletariat on an autonomous class basis with no relation *even to you*.

It is a useless bluff just to say: We put you both on the same level, one not a millimetre above the other and in one go we'll make you both fall like ninepins with the same ball.

The Left must defend itself from the stupid accusation of not being able to make sense of history and of mumbling abstract theses: they must prove that it is the others who have not understood history.

After the period of national liberation which settled that any alliance should be pitilessly condemned, the explanation of capitalism's survival had to be posed, not through the discovery of recipes such as the leading role of the State in the economy, but in the imperial relations of the great industrial apparatuses and in the continuing existence, not of territorial invasions of, nor of defeats in wars but of a State apparatus (the committee representing capitalist interests, as Marx rightly said, whether or not the State manages firms and shops) which is historically the most *continuous and persistent.*

Undoubtedly the concentration of power in Moscow is also an obstacle barring the way to revolution not only as the capital of proletarian corruption but also as a physical force in itself. But it has only been around for 34 years. Its territory and peoples are a mixture of social and economic types.

Germany and Japan are prostrate, France and Italy have been tremendously shaken. England itself is in a serious crisis.

And this is what makes America key. Another few years and the police of the UN will be effective and only a few minutes from every part of the world.

If possible we could drag the Big Moustache out of Moscow and put in his place say, in order not to offend anyone, Alfa: Truman who is already thinking about it will arrive within five minutes.

Have I made myself clear? If that is not the case then this means I myself have become stupid. This is not so serious, from the point of view of my dialectical Marxist convictions and not from voluntarism. I will do that little text, have no doubt.

[Third Letter] Onorio to Alfa 23 July 1951

I am replying, and in the same tone, as you wished.

The first observation which I am compelled to make is on the somewhat … sour tone of your letter which the content, and perhaps the form, of my observations have unwittingly provoked. In writing to you I started from concern about how the international groups, for whom the address is intended, would respond to our way of posing if not resolving, but at least defining the limits of the objective and subjective possibilities, of the problems of the international revival of revolutionary groups.

Agreed about the "political" sense – are you happy now? – that led you to give a defined and, in a certain sense negative, value to the address. This is more appropriate if we don't want to put off those who are coming closer to us and possibly could join us. But I don't agree with your method of argument, even when it is polite, which has the need at times to create arguments which are sometimes fictitious and at others, completely arbitrary. You give these opinions your own meaning, and the way you engage in combat gives the impression that your formulations are the real or hidden opinions of those who contradict you. It's fine to follow the thread of your own argument but take into account sometimes, and in an objective manner, what those you are discussing with are really saying.

I'll follow the order of your letter of 9 July.
America as Concentration No. 1? The formulation is right on the condition that it is understood that international capitalism taken as a single whole, even if differentiated by unequal development, has in America *"the greatest metropolitan concentration of capital, of forces of production and of power."*

But where do we get to when we translate this on to the level of tactics and political strategy? We get to your statement that

> *"America is above all way beyond the rest and in all probability will win in any future conflict [who would be able to stop it, I would add, and to what purpose?!] so it can certainly intervene anywhere an anti-capitalist revolution is victorious."*

Defeat today might come about like that. But so what? Should for this reason proclaim that revolution in this or that country would be useless until the proletariat has done away with the state in Washington D.C.? We are not joking, even if what you write has to be understood historically.

I'll go back to what I said before on this argument.

> *"The proletarian revolution strikes its class enemies when and how it can, wherever they appear weakest."*

Do I really have to add for your benefit that the revolution, even if it breaks out in Roccacannuccia[43], is always just one moment in the international revolution, yet you feel free to paraphrase just for me what Stalin would have said?

What is interesting though is the theoretical question raised here.

I would put it to you like this. Theoretically a revolutionary outbreak has to logically take place in some given concentration of power etc. etc. of the world capitalist order in which the accumulation of economic contradictions and the social antagonisms of capitalist domination have become more intense without the presumption, however, that this has *"economically reached the ultimate limits of its development"*.

At this point, instead of posing the problem as you do, in my view in a unilateral and static manner, of the suffocating intervention of the UN (and why not also that of the Cominform police who are no less interested in strangling the revolution?), we have to pose the other, historically more lively, problem which rests on the capacity and explosive potential of a first revolutionary outburst to spread in a world which is objectively ripe for socialism. It is the only way for the socialist revolution to concretely pose how to overcome Washington as well: in this sense and only in this sense *"the revolution is not its wasting time"*. But it surely is a waste if the revolution kicks its heels just waiting messianically for the conquest of power in the United States. The proletariat would certainly miss all the opportunities which the capitalist crisis will offer, no matter where, if it subordinates its international mission to the conquest of power in the United States.

On the basis of Bolshevik October we know that the dynamic towards the widening of revolutionary struggle inherent in any victorious radical overthrow of power, in part achieved, in part potential, cannot be measured scientifically in advance. It is a type of "atomic" reserve which every revolution carries within it. Does the psychological break widen it? The revolution breaks out, overcoming all obstacles with the world as its objective. In the opposite case the revolution is defeated, dies on its feet and "shrivels" as you say, and disappears. But this is the way, and it is the only way.

And let's come to the analysis and definition of Russian society today. You will note that on this subject I limit myself to the indirect formulation of questions and objections.

You write

> *"It is not accurate to say that the bourgeoisie was the protagonist in one period of capitalism and that the State is the protagonist today."*

Have you fished this inaccuracy from my writing perhaps and then formulated it in such a clumsy manner? Would it not have been more correct and even more useful in clarifying things if you were forced to take in to account even critically the importance of the objection I feel I have to try to put to you. I'll repeat what I wrote on the "economy and State" discussion.

> *"The tendency to an ever greater intervention of the state, which is characteristic in this economic period of the most highly industrialised countries, finds in the Soviet economy it's most complete, defined and organic expression etc. etc."*

Further on

"Being in the general line of development of monopoly capitalism enabled Russia to miss out more than one stage, thanks to the October Revolution, which allowed the most absolute centralisation of the economy within the orbit of the state and, thanks to the Stalinist counter-revolution, it made use of this enormous centralised economic potential to massively increase the power of the state and open the way to this latest capitalist experience."

The protagonist of this historic period is therefore the state whose economy reproduces, on a wider scale perhaps, the methods and characteristics which actually belong to capitalist production and distribution (wage labour, market, surplus value, accumulation etc…).

Forgive the length of the quotation but you compel me to show that no-one has confused and even less mixed up the terms "economy and State" and it is entirely useless to claim, as you do, that the State does not play a leading role in economic activity. It would have been better if you had instead refuted my argument.

The formula of the monopolistic period and state capitalism is extremely vague? But it is not mine and before anything else it was Lenin who stated that state capitalism, compatible with the dictatorship of the proletariat, had the task of acting as an intermediary between soviet power and the countryside and to establish their alliance. This was also Lenin who thought state capitalism was the dominant form of the soviet economy. This was 1921. In 1925 we turn to the words of Sokolnikov, a conscientious and honest witness:

"Our foreign trade is carried out like a state capitalist enterprise; our internal trade companies are equally state capitalist enterprises and the State Bank is in the same way a State enterprise. At the same time our monetary system is infused with the principles of the capitalist economy."

And from 1925 on? In *"Towards Capitalism or Towards Socialism?"* Trotsky wrote:

"In the face of the world capitalist economy the Soviet State behaves like a gigantic private owner."

Furthermore State industry united in a single trust is then effectively defined as *"the trust of trusts"*. It is thus a matter of knowing, the work cited comes from 1925, if *"with the development of the productive forces the capitalist tendency will increase at the expense of the socialist tendency"*. Recent history has proved the decisive prevalence of the tendency based on the commodity economy, which is, in short, capitalist.

If at this point the revolution shrivels, this does not mean that the trustified economy controlled by the State and with which the State gives it body has to decentralise and return to individual capitalism and its competitive regime. The instruments created by the technological evolution of the nationalised economy which should work for a more rapid realisation of socialism are, in fact, used to push on towards capitalism.

What do I mean when I say that the State gives substance to the trustified economy? I mean the tendency of imperialism to form that State which Lenin called the *rentier* State, the State of the usurers, where the bourgeoisie live by exporting capital and clipping *coupons*. Such a phenomenon, very visible in the US economy through the notable predominance of financial capitalism is common to the Russian economy itself even if it operates within a more restricted zone of influence.

> *"The world is divided into a small group of usurer States and a huge mass of debtor States."* (Lenin)

Manager State? Entrepreneur State? State subject to the economy? We are not talking about these but of considering certain phenomenon belonging to this phase of the economy which is financial capital, one of the levers of command manoeuvred mainly by the State, the policy of its export as an instrument of world domination, the organisation of a part of the economy on a permanent basis as a war economy, with the maintenance of two permanent armies, that of the bureaucrats and that of the military. All these phenomena come together in the State, the only unitary and potentially centralised organisation which can, and knows how to, resolve all the economic contradictions and social antagonisms whenever they reach their sharpest points in terms of force, violence and war. There is enough here, it seems to me, to show the imperialist State to be something more than its function as the representative committee of capitalist interests.

And like any capitalist phenomenon, even this one, the line of Marxist interpretation goes from the economy to the State and not vice versa. That capitalism still exists, and the apparatus of the most continuous and persistent State in history remains, is open to verification through the critical examination of Marxists. Those who have anything to say on this should say it …

And we thus arrive at the ruling class in Russia. I asked myself and continue to ask myself: who is the new class in Russia which exercises its own dictatorship via the State? For my part I limited myself to the real and historically irrefutable statement that

> *"The enormous power of the soviet state cannot have failed to concretely resolve the problem of a homogenous and strong ruling class through the consciousness which it has of its own being, and of the historic function which it is called upon to carry out."*

I can only agree about what you say on the role of the bureaucracy but your formula of a *"hybrid coalition and fluid association etc"* excludes from the present State the existence of a historically defined class and fits perfectly with your other formula of an economy which *tends* to capitalism. If it is tending towards capitalism it means that in Russia there is an economy that is not yet capitalist through which the ruling class expressing it *is tending* itself to become capitalist, and is not yet capitalist.

That the peasant economy *is tending* for the most part towards capitalism, I can agree; but that the trustified economy of the State tends to capitalism, absolutely no. It is this characteristically capitalist economic reality which inevitably produces the ruling class which is appropriate to it.

And here, it seems to me, is the key to all your thinking on the Russian problem. As a result, a socialist revolution in that country compared to the United States is not so urgent for you. Up to this point I don't think that the terms of our conversation have lacked clarity even if we have gone beyond the concerns of the international address.

[Fourth Letter] Alfa to Onorio 31 July 1951

I am replying to your letter of 22-23 July. I accept your proposal to remove any sharpness of tone.

First of all I also eliminate the accusation of having distorted your theses by formulating them in an exaggerated and erroneous way and I will force myself to return to your formulations and quotations just as you formulated them. It is not a bad method to attribute opinions which are slightly false to someone who contradicts you, rather it is a useful Marxist method, when it leads to greater clarity of important points, and especially when some elements, even at the highest level, have not taken them in after a great deal of time. I still say that I am a humble repeater and no more but I believe I have assimilated such a method well. Obviously, if the point made is a good one it is not so serious to have attributed to another a thesis that is not strictly theirs: in polemics democracy is of no interest to us. We don't have to win points for scholastic merit like in a school and still less make a general assessment to see who is best, because we have gone beyond that stage. A made-up dispute can be useful in taking things forward and, at times, the solution to an equation cannot be found by following normal procedures but by writing a deliberately false formula. Meanwhile no one has gone to gaol. Thus 'the bourgeoisie previously played a role whilst the State has now replaced it', are not words you sign up to, however there is a huge, more or less conscious, prejudice in circulation and it is useful to demolish it, a job that we can do together and does not redound to the merit or fame of any one author, etc.

And now some remarks. When I speak of an important capitalist centre of power which might rush to stamp out any attempt at revolution, I did not mean to forbid such attempts or to make a hierarchy of such attempts. I meant above all to highlight that the political movement, which has been allied to this centre of power in all the most decisive phases of its rise to hegemony, must be judged as counter-revolutionary by militant workers now, and always, even when in political debate it adopts theoretically communist and class positions which are no more than a joke. This is the point: for now we cannot carry out any attempt, neither in Pittsburgh nor in Casale. We have to work to rectify the approach of the class for tomorrow and the day after tomorrow. Why did I say we would see the UN and not the Cominform here? First of all the Cominform countries are in the UN. In second place, if I turn round I see the silhouette of *Mount Olympus*[44] and not that of a Soviet ship. I am absolutely convinced that troops will also land from that and I don't mind admitting it.

For the present, I have stopped to ask why you see the definition of the transitional phases of the Russian economy from one social type to another as the most important thing, and after that I will clarify an ambiguity which perhaps I unintentionally provoked on the "meaning" of these transitional tendencies, or rather, this series of transitions.

The three following questions don't form a single whole: is the Russian economy going in the right direction? Are the Russian Communist Party and the International following the right policy? Does the Russian state have the right international policy? I mean *right* in the revolutionary sense and I pose the questions generally as if one were posing them from 1919 to the present. It is clear that today we would answer in the negative to all three questions. But there is no condition which obliges us to reply to all three with a "yes" or a "no" and thus the economic issue is not decided by the other two.

As usual I will explain using historical examples. England's anti-Jacobin war and its support for the feudal emigrés. Which was the most progressive bourgeois economy in the world? England. Which was the country where the development of capitalism was not threatened by feudal counter-revolution. Idem (the same). But what was the English Government's policy towards the struggle in France? Counter-revolutionary, no less than that of Austria or Russia, where the aristocracy were in power. What was the foreign policy of the English Government? Counter-revolutionary, it attempted to stop the Convention and Napoleon. We have not replied yes – yes – yes or no – no – no. We replied yes – no – no.

The 1917 revolution in Russia and the first, however primitive, communist measures. Communist struggle throughout the world, international struggle against the Germans and the Entente on every front: three revolutionary positions, yes – yes – yes. Was it an error to have started the world and European revolution in the least capitalist country only for it to end in defeat? We have said at least a hundred times that we wouldn't dream of making that criticism!

The social and economic retreat of 1921 and abandonment of certain socialist forms (the strictly economic point later). We, all of us on the left, approved the justifications for the international revolutionary strategy: a step backwards to catch our breath: reply no – yes – yes. That is the internal social economy goes backward, the revolutionary struggle goes forward.

After Lenin's death tactical deviations began from 1922 to, let's say 1926, but there was no alliance with any bourgeois country in the world because they were all struggling against Russia: we in the Left were not happy with party policy: our reply no – no – yes.

Further degeneration, both in the domestic economy and in party policy, which became collaborationist and opportunist and in which the foreign policy of the Russian state finally made alliances with capitalists. We have finally reached no – no – no.

I wanted to establish that the yes and the no of the internal economic process does not automatically determine, by itself alone, the other two replies. The three responses taken together depend on an understanding of the international historic framework, in Marxist terms, dialectically.

This takes away a lot of the importance from the problem which seems to you – or seems to many – to be the key problem: what is the nature of the present Russian economy, of the new class etc. Its not that this is not an important problem it is only that its solution does not resolve all the other issues. Like the English economy, which was the most advanced in 1793 whilst it pursued the most reactionary foreign policy, so it could be that a country which had evolved social and economic characteristics of socialism, could have a bourgeois party policy and make war. Whatever the truth about the economic process of Russia and its real "direction" the party and international policy of the Stalinists is equally fetid.

That is why, in the appeal to the workers, it is not so important for me to say: in Russia Citizen Capitalistov, at such and such an address, does nothing and pampers himself with caviar, vodka and Rubens paintings but: the policy of dissolving the [Communist – translator] parties, so the Americans and English could make their war all the better, stank as did the policy of the partisan fronts.

And now to your central point: state capitalism. This is exactly what one finds in Trotsky, Sokolnikov, Lenin and, of the rest, Marx and Engels a century ago: look at the *Fili*[45] one after another where I proved it some time ago. Now we can see what state capitalism is. But you go further, you speak of a state economy and the "*most absolute concentration of the economy within the ambit of the state*". Now such a formula, I don't say deserves many years in prison but I say stop to think that, from a Marxist point of view, the following terms are not well presented: society – production – economy – State. And now I'll go over it and in doing so I don't want to belittle anyone.

Let's start by establishing another central point. Let's allow for a series of the following economic types: a capitalism of free competition and personally owned firms – a capitalism of trusts, monopoly – financial parasitic capitalism – state direction of the economy – the statification of industrial and banking firms. Let's then take the series of political power relationships: bourgeois parliamentary democracy – imperialism and totalitarian capitalism – revolutionary proletarian power – degenerating proletarian power – degenerated, and therefore capitalist, proletarian power (without *a third class* and not because there are only two classes in modern society).

So *I said* that the two series are not in parallel: they don't have a one to one relationship as we say in mathematics. Any category of the first series can, in time x and in place y, coincide with any category in the second series.

I will begin to explain. What is it that we cannot get into the heads of democrats and libertarians, our *number one key Marxist point*: the dictatorship? What is the central argument? It is not only possible but inevitable that an hour, a year or five years after the destruction of bourgeois power, an economic cell, an enterprise structure of a bourgeois type will survive: we say one to mean eventually also the whole system. In these sectors of production there will not only be exploited wage workers but also a boss who appropriates a profit. Yet this does not take away from the fact that at the same time there is a full proletarian political power: it just means that the transformation of production has not yet reached that sector. It will be done later. Meanwhile the bourgeoisie is deprived of political and civil rights controlled, even if still tolerated, by the organs of the red dictatorship. And this? And is it for this alone that the dictatorship is justified and imposed? Fine. Therefore we can have a proletariat and revolutionary party in power which has good tactic at home and in the Communist International and at the same time a capitalist economic zone which even might include private enterprise.

Vice-versa, with a purely bourgeois power such as that in England we can have a totally statified industrial sector, or rather one which has not only passed from personal ownership to a limited company then to an enterprise controlled by a trust to end up with the type in which the State is the owner and entrepreneur of the firm thus it is not just a concession, but it directs it economically, like for example the Tobacco Manufacture in Italy: every worker is an employee of the State. As I have said on numerous occasions, we have even more real communist organisational types under capitalist power, for example, the fire service: when something is burning no-one pays to put out the fire; if nothing is burning the firecrew are kept on all the same.

I say all this to oppose the idea, whoever the author, that points to the successive stages: private capitalism, state capitalism as a lower form of socialism, higher form of socialism or communism.

State capitalism is not a semi-socialism but a real and proper capitalism, it is the very outcome of capitalism according to the Marxist theory of concentration and it condemns the free market theory of a permanent regime of production in which the admirable game of competition forever puts within reach of all a new slice of capital.

The ownership of the means of production is not enough to discriminate between capitalism and socialism (see *Property and Capital*[46]) but we need to consider the whole economic phenomenon, or rather, who disposes of the product and who consumes it.

Pre-capitalism, the economy of individual producers: the product is that of the independent labourer; everyone consumes what they produce. This doesn't deny that examples of surplus production and therefore surplus labour are made to the detriment of multitudes of workers (at times united with strength in numbers but without the modern division of production) divided by caste, order and privileged power.

Capitalism: associated labour (in Marx *social* labour), division of labour produced at the will of the capitalist and not the worker, who receives money to buy on the market as much as he needs to maintain his strength. The whole mass of produced objects pass through the monetary form on the journey from production to consumption.

The lower stage of socialism. The worker receives from the unitary socio-economic organisation a fixed quantity of products which he needs in life and cannot have more of them. Money has ended but consumer goods, which can neither be accumulated nor exchanged, still exist. The ration card? In the lower stage of socialism it is the card for everyone without the use of money and without a market.

The higher stage of socialism and communism. In every sector the ration card has a tendency to be abolished and everyone obtains as much as they need. Someone wants to go to 100 cinema shows in a row? They can do so, even today. Will you telephone the fire brigade after you have set the house on fire? You can do it today but under communism there will be no insurance. However, then and now the mental health service is run according to the pure communist economy, i.e. free and unlimited.

Recapitulation:

Precapitalism: economy without money and with work complementing money. Parcelled out production.

Capitalism: Economy with totalitarian employment of money. Social production.

Lower stage of socialism: Economy without money and with ration cards. Idem (i.e. the same social production)

Higher stage of socialism or communism: Economy without either money or ration card. Idem.

State capitalism, which it would be cretinous to call "state socialism", remains entirely within capitalism. Everyone becomes a state wage worker. Surplus value, exploitation, etc persist. **You** say so, and that's exactly right but it is not enough to see things in these terms, they must be located in their precise locations of time and space etc.

Before I come to the process in Russia, a further word on things I have often said or rather repeated in my articles.

The payment of money wages defines capitalism. Surplus value is only a consequence deduced by Marx from it in argument, dialectically, **even and also** including the gratuitous assumption that exchange everywhere is always free and equal. There is no such thing as a wage labour regime which gives the undiminished fruits of labour in money to the labourer (he taught that to Lassalle). For two principal reasons: only commercial methods lead to capitalist accumulation and exploitation (C-M-C, M-C-M^1 etc); a deduction is always indispensable for social ends; maintenance, depreciation, improvements through unceasing investment in newly manufactured goods which become production goods.

In a commercial atmosphere there cannot be social advance without class exploitation. But the fact is as follows: the amount of surplus value the capitalist minority materially rakes off **is not** the preponderant phenomenon. It is the deduction ostensibly for social ends which becomes abnormal, mistaken, disproportionate and destructive.

The average working day throughout the world is ten hours.

The capitalists rake off half an hour.
Capitalism wolfs down six and half hours
The worker gobbles at best three hours.

Under state capitalism, and more in appearance than anything else, we get rid of the half hour. This isn't important. But there is a greater concentration of the conditions which make it tremendously more difficult to recover the other six hours which have become seven or more. It would be more socialist to tie up all the capitalists and send them to Tahiti to exploit themselves for an hour and administer the other nine hours: after a short while we would need to work less hours a day.

Therefore in a certain sense I can agree with you that, starting from different points the capitalist countries and Russia have reached comparable situations as far as their economic tissue is concerned where the state accumulates, manages, and invests capital which has no private ownership. The concentration of power makes it easier to capitalise sectors which are still economically pre-capitalist. Good. However the power of the state never ceases to be used for class ends even from the beginning when it was not *theoretically* interested in the economy. (A bourgeois economy arises on the basis of the free exchange of equivalents but this is not possible without a concrete force which is ready to strike at those who tend to exchange non-equivalents in the bourgeois legal sense; therefore the factor of the State is *always* decisive).

In bourgeois countries you will recall the description of Lenin which was valid right up until the First World War. Good here too. Let's turn to the creditor and debtor countries (not states) which invest abroad and the real explanation of parasitism. In the modern form this does not consist of coupon clippers or *rentiers* but of *big businessmen* and, as ever, entrepreneurs: but we are no longer talking of entrepreneurs in production who work on small margins but of very big businessmen with colossal waste and very frequent changes of personnel.

To my mind dirigisme[47] and modern state capitalism leave greater space than in the past for the brigandage of private initiatives or groups, in the class solidarity which the bourgeoisie has socially and politically had since it appeared, an ever more global solidarity, even in war.

Here is an "analysis" on which we could do well to work. Only that the mechanism can be, let's say, in Siberia, or in a group making profits in Canada … via Tangiers or somewhere else.

I'll finish for now by looking at the process in Russia. I began with the remark that under the Tsar capitalism was only present in heavy and war industry: at bottom capitalism is born in a State form (the arsenals of absolute monarchies etc) the private factories only come along later…

The bourgeois democratic revolution would have been sufficient to give a greater impetus to the development of the capitalist tendency in all the other backward sectors of the economy: peasant, patriarchal, Asiatic etc. etc, artisanal, trading and such like. Naturally the October Revolution, carried out mainly by the industrial proletariat of the large cities, pushed the entire economy of the country further forward and therefore from then on at least nine tenths of pre-bourgeois Russian society *tend to capitalism* and could not tend towards socialism just through this mechanism.

But I spoke about that tenth of the economy which attempted to become socialist and then *had to take a step back towards capitalism.* Have these tendencies now all ended, and is it now capitalist? We could admit it but only from that point when it gave up any attempt to wait for the world revolution: the counter-revolutionary position was reached even if in Moscow ... the firemen cost nothing.

In 1919-20 in Leningrad[48] and Moscow you could take the tram free, that is to say not just workers going to and from work but anyone who wanted to get on didn't have to pay for a *ticket* or show a card. You didn't pay on the train either but you needed a ticket from a soviet organisation. The lower stage of socialism in this case.

The factory worker got a lot of things in kind amongst which was bread which was taken from the countryside even by force. Money had no value; everyone got a little money and bought something on the black market.

When NEP began Lenin explained; it's no good, we have to legalise the market, allow the peasantry, after paying tax in kind, to bring goods to the provincial market to exchange for industrial products, and pay factory workers in money. It's useless to go on whilst waiting for *the world revolution*, and even in the big centres and in heavy industry we have to extinguish the little socialism that the Russian economy allowed, and fall back to capitalism. We don't have bourgeois bosses in the factories or their shares quoted on the London Stock Exchange. Which, Lenin said, perhaps makes this a socialist factor? This is still capitalism, but of the State. Even if it is a proletarian state which governs here the thing smells more of the rule of a bourgeois state.

Re-read your quotations and you will see that they correspond with what I am saying. Ever since then, it has accumulated and invested, spreading industrialism and capitalist potential always on the backs of the workers: you are right. It always takes the same form: capitalism. Of the State should we add? All right.

Wherever it is, and wherever the economic form of the market exists, capital is a *social* force. It is a *class* force. It has at its beck and call the political *State*. Its interests become ever more international, even when the agonising struggle of the central states brings about war. They form an impersonal network, have their own dynamic inertia which moves according to their own laws.

By making the idea of the present situation of such forces in the Russian context concrete I believe I am saying something which goes beyond the phrase "state capitalism" which in itself says *nothing*.

[Fifth Letter] Onorio to Alfa 6 October 1951

I am taking up the conversation at the point where your letter of 31 July left it and I have drafted some summary notes by way of conclusion. My criticism is addressed mainly to your statement that the revolution would be "wasting its time" if it had not first sought to do away with the most important centre of capitalism, universally identified today as the state of Washington D.C.

Here you agree with me, and you had no choice, that you don't mean to put a ban on revolutionary attempts elsewhere or to create a hierarchy of such attempts. In truth we Marxists don't talk of "prohibition" but of recognising that a revolutionary outbreak can come anywhere in the capitalist world and that it expresses – this is the main point – a capacity and explosive potential for extension which is the basis of revolutionary socialist strategy that leads it to spread abroad and to try to "do away with" the state of Washington D.C. All this has to be understood historically and not in order to avoid discussing its validity, both theoretically and politically. It isn't very convincing as a political argument aiming at the revolutionary preparation of those proletarians who have to judge the political trajectory of Soviet Russia (which allied with America in the most decisive period of its rise to hegemony) as counter-revolutionary. There can be no agreement with this argument which, put in this context seems like a purely political expedient to avoid the real problem which is the profound capacity for extension of any victorious revolution wherever the initial revolutionary victory takes place.

Incidentally I remember reading in our *"Battaglia"* something on this subject which tried to take an original position between our two viewpoints which will cease to diverge as soon as you accept that the revolution can break out in the face of a proletarian assault wherever capitalism seems weakest. This thesis, supported by the writer in *"Battaglia"*, is a significant enough example of the way in which the problem of revolution is posed: it starts with a political polemic in place of a dialectical examination.

In this the anti-Stalinist revolution is posed as *"conditio sine qua non"* because it makes the defeat of the state of Washington D.C possible. But it does not ask if this revolution, in so far as it is the work of the proletariat, resolves the fundamental class problem which is that of the destruction of the capitalist state which then allows the capitalist economy to pass to the level of socialist production and distribution. It isn't mentioned because whoever wrote the article believes in a revolution devoid of material premises essential in a Marxist conception.

This is a throwback to motives of a purely idealist and voluntarist type which we thought had been definitely overcome at least within our small vanguard. The Anti-Stalinist revolution, due to the fact that it will be carried out by the proletariat, will have all the characteristics of an anti-capitalist one, otherwise it will just be reduced to a banal episode of a palace revolution and a mere changing of the guard.

And whilst we are applying dialectical method I'll pick up the thread of our conversation to say what I think about your "method" of dealing with the dialectic in history. It seems to me that your game of yes/no contradictions is totally devoid of formal dialectics; they may have some demonstrative value in the historical examples you quote in relation to your argument but they don't fully satisfy the need for a dialectical evaluation of the revolutionary motives of the nascent bourgeoisie. The facts which you draw out of the British experience seem formally correct, but anyone who thinks and believes in a type of correspondence, which is not just temporal, between the movement of things in the subsoil and the movement of the social and political forces in the superstructure, thinks and believes according to the precepts of a mechanical determinism which is contrary to the historical materialism meant by Marx. It is, in other words, more "historical" than "materialist". I remind you with Bukharin that

> *"…any contradiction between the productive forces and the economy are quickly smoothed out, it rapidly exercises its influence on the superstructure, then the superstructure in its turn on the economy and the productive forces and the circle starts again without interruption."*

In short we are not just talking about grasping the contradiction between an evolving English economy with a capitalist character and a corresponding anti-Convention and anti-Napoleon[49] policy of parties and Government.

The unfolding of the English industrial revolution had posed a problem of a political and social organisation as a revolutionary choice in bourgeois dress, whose progress was affirmed and measured by the quantity of economic, social and political forces of the old order which it defeated, and on their material capacity for resistance.

You asked yourself if the English industrial revolution had then been only English?

And so can we accept what you state that "all" the English superstructural forces were counter-revolutionary? For the most part what was dominant in English foreign policy was the need to struggle for hegemony on a continent which France threatened. This is very easy to explain but to say that it was in "toto", no. In any case the struggle on a political level between the forces of the dying Ancien Regime and the new liberal forces expressed by the industrial revolution did not mean dialectically that the bourgeois revolt would succeed. The movement of the Enlightenment had its first formulation in England after the Revolution of 1688 and it ended with the storming of the Bastille which was on the other hand a response, the first of a series of revolutionary responses, to the internationally posed demands of a nascent capitalism. However, the line of historical development of the liberal movement is easily identifiable and we would fail to understand, both in its totality and its contradictions, the advance of England in the modern bourgeois world if we undervalued the vast and progressive conflict between the new and increasing forces of the liberal movement and the Ancien Regime, between the defenders of "*habeas corpus*" and the return of absolutism, between the world of strong medieval leftovers and the age of religious conflict, of the political privileges of landed property and the world of industry and commerce, the policy of the Government was by force of necessity counter-revolutionary in regard to the France of both the Convention and Napoleon.

And it is along this line of dialectical interpretation that we will arrive at a consciousness of the real reasons which were at the heart of the first workers' movements: angry reactions against machines seen as the cause of unemployment, and the rise of the first workers' unions which would lead to a large number of strikes.

There is, in a word, an expanding and assertive capitalist economy with a corresponding ruling class, the bourgeoisie, whose policy is both liberal and reactionary at the same time, progressive but also prudently conservative. Everyone knows that in every society, in the to and fro between the progressive and reactionary and in all historical periods, there is a tendency for tradition to prevail.

Some further observations on your way of applying the dialectic to the experience of Soviet Russia. You write:

> *"The social and economic retreat of 1921 and abandonment of certain socialist forms (the strictly economic point later). We, all of us on the left, approved the justifications for the international revolutionary strategy: a step backwards to catch our breath: reply no – yes – yes. That is the internal social economy goes backward, the revolutionary struggle goes forward."*

The replies you give "no – yes – yes", can make sense if referring to the entire subjective condition of our political struggle back then. But if we had to respond to the same questions today there is no doubt that we would respond "no" to all three, i.e. it is not true that the social economy in the USSR was retreating and the revolutionary struggle was advancing. Now we know that the socialised economy within Russia was retreating and the revolutionary struggle did not advance after the death of Lenin onwards neither in the fatherland … of socialism nor anywhere else.

The truth is that we of the Left showed that we were against the policy of the Party but we did not worry enough about linking the reasons for the decline of the world proletarian revolution to the retreat from socialism, and its disappearance from the economic and social organisations of the first proletarian revolution. The fault lies with us alone for preferring to turn ourselves in to assertors of the dialectic of words in place of a dialectic of things.

Agreed, there is nothing automatic in all this, there is only a backward development on the level of the superstructure towards bourgeois practices, the reflection of a return to a truly capitalist mode of production. This is why the hypothesis you have formulated is dominated by idealism.

"Like the English economy which was the most advanced in 1793 whilst it pursued the most reactionary foreign policy so it could be that a country which had evolved social and economic characteristics of socialism could have a bourgeois party policy and make war."

If we are dealing with a present possibility, logic demands you refer directly to the Russian experience, if on the other hand we are dealing with a future possibility, the hypothesis is of no interest to us, because it has abandoned a Marxist analysis.

Finally, I freely acknowledge how our initially divergent arguments on the evaluation of state capitalism have, as is natural, come closer. It's only that the old police function of the state, rather than its interest in the economy, has greater emphasis in your vision of the bourgeois world, whilst in mine the state increases its power to the maximum, especially to protect the economy which it concentrates in itself against the competing and contradictory forces which have increased on both a national and international scale.

Since we both consider that state capitalism *"is to be found entirely and totally within capitalism"* we also draw from this the same conclusion on the process in Russia. For my part I hold to this with your own words which, in their turn, sum up what I have been writing to you on the Russian economy as state capitalist.

"Ever since then, it has accumulated and invested, spreading industrialism and capitalist potential always on the backs of the workers: you are right. It always takes the same form: capitalism. Of the State should we add? All right.

Wherever it is, and wherever the economic form of the market exists, capital is a social force. It is a class force. It has at its beck and call the political State."

These are precise terms until 1900, the epoch which we usually make the start of the period of imperialist expansion. These terms remain true and current, even if, taken in isolation, incomplete, when the evolution of capitalism confers on the State the function of taking over from private initiative as the terminal point of such an evolution. It would be worth the effort to document the present development of certain sectors of the American economy to see this phenomenon, on which bourgeois observers have already remarked, in reality, in the characteristic realisation of state capitalism attributed to the powerful personality of the Kaiser. In talking of state economy it's not me who is going too far. These are the facts of the economy which is so dynamically ahead of us that sometimes we fall back on old economic schemas because when facts don't match with history we cease to be Marxists. We would not be true to our revolutionary understanding and "culture" if we too were backward on these issues.

We are not just dealing with a more or less sharp debate over a theoretical point but making clear and defining the character of the present period of capitalist development which poses the problem of a particular tactical and strategic vision for the revolutionary party and not some set of ... Trappist monks.

For Russia, which can't be left out of this reality, this is particularly important. According to your view its economy is tending towards capitalism; you say that nine-tenths of Russian pre-bourgeois society tends there, as is now that tenth of the economy which had attempted to become socialist and is now going backwards. Let's recognise that the tendency of the nine-tenths is on the right lines but what of the other tenth, even in the supposition that it was on the way to socialism, let's say though an inferior version, it cannot now tend to capitalism because it structurally cannot, in my view, return to the private entrepreneur but carries on functioning with the characteristics of a centralised economy within the ambit of the State which appears today as the "natural outlet of capitalism according to the Marxist theory of concentration". It is in this real world that we find the motives of a party and state policy which stinks, and which has no valid dialectical connection with either a historical or revolutionary point of view.

I don't want to conclude these remarks without giving my impression on what you have said, or rather, the way you have said it. What do I mean? When I re-read your writings after some time the strange feeling of astonishment and dissatisfaction gleaned from the first reading was still present and perhaps even more explicit. What is disconcerting is that there is in your writings a central motif, a fuzziness which doesn't fully make itself clear, and around it all a fringe of sparkling polemics, where it is not difficult to discern a tendency to minimise and make accommodations on any issue.

This central motif is a product of your conviction that the Soviet economy in its backward march towards capitalism, has not yet brought this u-turn to a conclusion, in simple terms it has not fully returned to capitalism.

All the rest is derived from this barely stressed conviction, in the formulation of a hypothetical country with evolved social characteristics which has a bourgeois policy of party and war, in the exhausting research into French and English history to find valid examples as proof, and finally the theory of Capitalist Concentration No. 1, the USA towards which all revolutionary efforts must be directed whilst the Russian concentration is to be dealt with later, and in a totally subordinate fashion thanks to the Proletarian Revolution.[50]

Why do I insist so much on this particular aspect of your interpretation? Because of the consequences which can be drawn from it on a more directly political level. In truth you don't accept that we treat the USA and Russia equally and not just at the moment.

It is impossible for the revolutionary party not to practice a policy of equidistance, especially if it is in a period where war has already been declared between a fully developed capitalist country like the USA, and a Russia which you make out is tending towards capitalism. It could be the theoretical premise for new ambiguous experiences. In every way this would profoundly disturb the strategic vision of the revolutionary party in the course of the next imperialist war.

If this final judgement is inspired by the demon of polemic I can only acknowledge it with pleasure.

Et de hoc satis.[51]

On the Union Question

Amongst the fundamental problems that the Internationalist Communist Party had to face following the end of the Second World War the union issue was among the most important. The validity of the work the party was called upon to develop on the level of demand struggles and within the union movement depended on a clear evaluation and definition of the role that the unions would play in the immediate post-war period. Alongside the differences on the unions which had developed in the Party Bordiga clarified his own thoughts in a letter which was later published in the "Pre-congress Bulletin 1952" with this explanation:

> "Comrade Bordiga has finally seen fit to specify in detail his thinking on the union question. The way that this letter/ document came to the Party would be irrelevant if not for the fact that, having been sent before the meeting of June 1, 1951 in Milan, it remained in the pockets of the recipient, in a Stalinist way, and was only brought to light later for reasons of force majeure." [52]

Bordiga's Letter of January 5, 1951

1) The current union situation is different from that of 1921, not only because of the absence of a strong Communist Party, but also due to the fact that the content of union activity has been progressively eliminated and bureaucratic functions are replacing rank and file action: assemblies, elections, party fractions in the unions. This applies to everything from professional staff to heads, etc. This disappearance, favourable to the interests of the capitalist class, follows the same narrative as those other factors: CLN-type corporatism, unions of the Di Vittorio[53] or Pastore[54]type. There is no reason to declare this process irreversible. If a strong Communist Party faces up to the capitalist offensive, if the proletariat openly distances itself from the (union) tactics of the National Liberation Committee (CLN), if it escapes the influence of the current Russian policy, then it is possible that at some time X and in some country Y class unions may resurface *ex novo* or by conquering existing unions. We cannot exclude this from a historical perspective. And these unions certainly will be formed during a period of advancing struggles, of a fight for the conquest of power. In both cases it is immaterial that D'Aragona[55], or Di Vittorio leads today, that does not stop our fraction's activity in the CGL.

2) Given the limited strength of the party, while this is not growing enough and we do not know if it will before or after the revival of non-political class organisations that have many members, the party could not nor should not proclaim a boycott of unions, factory organs and workers' struggles, nor submit on principle its own candidates' list in union elections in the factories nor, wherever there is a majority in support, use the slogan of boycott in workers' struggles, encouraging them not to vote, or not to belong to the union, nor to go on strike or other such things. Putting

it positively, in most cases, practical abstention not boycott.

3) In certain situations, wherever the balance of forces is favourable, we should never raise the slogan of boycott. We may or may not submit lists of our own, depending on the practical consequences anticipated, and in any case we spread our principles by means of the factory group formed by elements of the party, that emanates from the party and is subordinate to the party.

4) It is necessary to develop the propaganda of the history of unions, and in particular explain the tactics of the Communist International and the Communist Party of Italy in the favourable phase of the First World War, the Theses of Moscow and Rome, etc.., etc.., the history of the communist union fraction of the CGL, the railway union, etc. A principle: no intermediate bodies between the party and the class means no possibility of revolution. The party does not abandon these organs just because it is a minority in them. But in no case does it submit its principles and directives to the will of the majority under the pretext that they are "workers". This also applies to the Soviets. (See Lenin, Zinoviev, etc …).
Amadeo Bordiga, January 5, 1951.

What follows are some excerpts from Bordiga's letters and documents, which clearly demonstrate, especially with regard to the union issue, that Bordiga's "thinking" was struggling and shows some uncertainty. In any case it was far removed – at that time – from the position of boycotting strikes and indifference towards workers' struggles. In fact he was in favour of participating in such struggles, though always fighting the line imposed by the unions. It was these positions (boycott and indifference) that would characterise the behaviour of those who would be his supporters at the time of the 1952 split. And it should be noted that it was precisely the "union issue" which was the main stage for numerous twists and tactical stunts of the "new party" that the splitters went on to form, this time with Bordiga at their head.

"Today in Italy, given the small size of the party, you cannot raise the slogan that these organs [unions] must be conquered and always participate in their elections, but we cannot and must not raise the slogan of a general boycott. Ninety percent, maybe ninety-nine percent of the time, the numerical correlation of forces is such that the problem does not even arise. But where it does, you might think about participation in campaigns, with lists in some cases, and generally without accepting posts that you may possibly win, but always spreading our criticism and propaganda. The basis for this task is the workplace group and other groups of adherents to the party. It is the party going to the workplace, and not vice versa, they are not cells from below, but instruments of the party, which is organised on a territorial basis (the Left in 1925).

The Italian left has never confused parliamentary issues with unions, which are very different. In the latter it has always been in favour of participation, and never in

64

favour of boycott or departure."
A. Bordiga, February 2, 1951.

"The party does not include more than a part of the working class, the party leads the working class not only through teaching its doctrine, proselytising in favour of their organisation and the preparation of military actions, but also by participating in organs much larger than the party and accessible to all class members. This means that there are three levels (and this is most evident on the eve of the major events): the party, that according to the left is not vast, the proletarian organisations by their constitution, which only include workers regardless of their ideological adherence, and the class, which includes everyone, including those who are not organised."
A. Bordiga, February 2 1951.

"However the call to create another *couche*[56], related to other organs which 'constitutionally' do not only contain proletarians, but also elements of other classes (parliamentary bodies, etc…) is a DIFFERENT question, a pure manoeuvre. The first question which arises now is a central problem, if we do not solve it, there'll be no revolutionary class or class party, before, during or after the revolution."
A. Bordiga, February 2, 1951.

"As for unions, I have come to this conclusion: in the absence of an organ linking proletarian interests, the connective tissue between the vital centre of the party and the peripheral muscles of the class, the revolution is impossible. It has to be independently reborn, outside the influence of the ruling class, in new forms.

I would be in favour of Onorato's formula where he proposes to free the union movement from bourgeois oppression, but against his claim that this depends on workplace organs and not on 'external' organs of economic association. The union is a non-constitutional voluntary organisation and, and the bourgeoisie is trying to destroy this form."
A. Bordiga, April 15, 1951.

Damen to Bordiga on the Union Question[57]

It seems superfluous to point out once again my position on the "union-party" issue on the many points on which we agree completely, compared to the few, even rare cases where our analyses differ due, not just to a disagreement of principle, but because we see our experience differently as we have lived it differently.
Let's take them in order. Our agreement is complete in:
1) Rejecting the slogan, whether expressed, implicit or implemented, to boycott unions, workplace organs and workers' struggles.
2) Participating when our success is practically possible in elections to workplace committees, with or own list but in the end not taking the seats won.

3) Considering factory groups, which go from the party to the places of work and not the other way around, as the basis of our work.

4) Considering still valid the position of the left, which has always declared for participation and not boycott or departure, with regard to the union issue.

The agreement is not as complete when we take this participation from the factory to the union, in which we are virtually absent and therefore it is physically impossible to exert any influence. Our approach also differs on the problem of the reconquest of existing unions. You wrote: "If a strong Communist Party faces up to the capitalist offensive, if the proletariat openly distances itself from the (union) tactics of the National Liberation Committee, if it escapes the influence of the current Russian policy, then it is possible that at some time X and in some country Y class unions may resurface *ex novo* or by conquering existing unions. We cannot exclude this from a historical perspective. And these unions certainly will be formed during a period of advancing struggles, of a fight for the conquest of power."

I think that the current corporate union (who cares if fascist, communist or social democratic), due to its essential role in the revival of the capitalist system, is destined to continue until the end of the economic, social and political hardships of a dying capitalism, and will only be defeated when the assault of the revolutionary proletariat brings down the imperialist state. In such a period of advance and struggle for power the regroupment of proletarian forces won't wait for a repeat of the traditional unions, but will face up to the specific problems of power in new mass organisations with a more suitable structure than that of the unions (factory councils, or soviets or others, such as occurred in Russia and Germany) and under the direction of the revolutionary party,

Finally, on your hypothesis that extracting the proletariat from Russian influence necessarily involves their immediate and certain fall under American influence, an oscillation which depends on which of the two opposing poles of imperialism is more attractive. This is perhaps a historical period in which unions of all kinds will politically flourish, but in no way is it, nor can it be, a period of class unionism.

Currently, unions interest us, but not because we consider them as proletarian organs under bourgeois dictatorship, as you think, but because the masses are in them, which on one hand are unable to fend for themselves on the class terrain and on the other are constantly willing to be drawn into the realm of imperialist competition. That is where we must exercise our critical activity of class re-education and political orientation; such activity must be accompanied by our own union policy, to be developed in the workplace, and especially wherever the reaction of the union bureaucracy is less effective against party political free speech. In this sense, I think the need for regrouping proletarians on the terrain of absolute autonomy, no matter if few in number at the beginning, must always be the central concern of the party. This is the specific way to focus the significant and not too distant experience of our union fraction.

A Note on the Internal Crisis

I enclose the statement I sent to the E.C. which raises the problem of the crisis at the top of the party in real terms. We do not accept the experiments whose theoretical justification has led me and then comrade Bottaioli[58] to leave the EC. The issue that has divided us and still divides us is always to defend the political line adopted in Florence[59], voted for or not. Now, if the centre continues to have a different opinion, if it continues to believe that this can become detrimental to the organisation, I think it's time to raise the specific problem of the active defence of that political line, applying wherever physically possible, with or without the consent of the EC, a line which can be roughly summarised as follows:

1) To clearly reject any perspective that means leaving the unions, and the boycott of these organisms and their struggles
2) To participate in the struggle in the Internal Commissions, openly and with our own list, in the workplaces where it is materially possible to show our strength and not accept any posts that might be gained.
3) To reject without hypocrisy the policy that minimises the present and future tasks of the party and that restricts the field of possible activity based on concerns that have nothing to do with revolutionary militant activity.
4) To reactivate the organisational and political life of the party, starting from what it considers suitable for the revolutionary struggle, without running away from the responsibilities of this fight, but facing up to them depending on our objectives, the immediate situation and the opposing political forces dialectically reflected in the dynamics of class conflict.

O. Damen, March 14, 1951.

Points of Disagreement with the
1952 "Platform" Drafted by Bordiga

During a party meeting held in Florence (8-9 December 1952), Bordiga presented a document in a schematic form which focused on the tasks and activities of the Party. The pretext for it was that, as a basis for the organisation, the document affected all adherents to the Party. The more "ambiguous" points were discussed in the journal Battaglia Comunista *(No. 5, March 1952) and are reproduced below.[The numbers and titles are taken from the original draft by Bordiga – translators' note]*

With the following critical notes we aim to clarify our points of disagreement with the "platform" which we refer to in the document. It should be understood that, in principle, we agree with the other points of the platform. We think that in this way we may specify the most serious reasons for the differences that weigh on the life of the party, and which must be resolved at the next congress.

I. Doctrine

1. - "Theoretical basis: Marxist historical materialism."

The acceptance of historical materialism does not imply, nor should it imply, the rigid acceptance of a body of doctrine since its interpretation is always open and alive. That would close our eyes to reality and could cause our vanguard movement some problems in the future, considering that among us there are those who do not accept the Marxist dialectic as a complete view of the world and of life, or accept it in an idealistic or deterministic way, i.e., "externally", to the extent that they are inspired by a mechanistic scientism. In short, there are those who sense it and translate it historically, putting more emphasis on the "historical" than the "materialism".

"Our doctrine, Engels said, is not a dogma, but a guide to action. This classic formula strongly emphasises this aspect of Marxism with extraordinary conciseness, that we lose sight of at every moment. And thus we turn Marxism into something one-sided, deformed and dead, emptying it of its essence and undermining its fundamental theoretical bases: the dialectic, the doctrine of the multiform historical evolution full of contradictions; weakening its close practical relations with each era, which may change with each new historical twist." (Lenin).

3. - "The proletarian dictatorship is exercised by the party."

This statement is valid and politically and theoretically correct, despite the terrible recent Russian experience, provided that we consider that the party and its governing bodies, which in fact exercise the dictatorship, should act as a part of the class, in unison with the interests, struggles and historical objectives of the entire proletariat, until classes and the state disappear. Historically, the dictatorship is that of the proletariat and not of the party, in the sense that it is the proletariat, as a class that has come to power, which channels and focuses in "its" party and crystallises in it the reasons, the strength and will that feeds the proletarian dictatorship. Beyond this, lies Stalinism, i.e. the dictatorship of the state (Party-State) which replaces the proletariat and throws it back to oppression, reversing the wheel of revolution.

II. The General task of the Class Party

2. - *"Fighting for the victory of bourgeois revolutions over the feudal system to boost capitalist production is a dialectical necessity."*

But this fight means that the revolutionary party actively participates in the ideology, organisation and policy of the bourgeois movement that is now penetrating economically backward areas, i.e. dragging these areas out of the extra-capitalist sphere for inclusion in its production process. It is not, therefore, about fighting so capitalism can increase its "greed" and its natural inclination to extend into backward areas. Capitalism is merely obeying the logic of its structure, the dynamics of its internal contradictions, the drive of its interests, which is clearly demonstrated by the fact that, thanks to this activity, not only are there very few extra-capitalist areas left, but they are currently unable to provide a sufficient and safe reserve as markets of consumption.

It is not, therefore, about fighting for the victory of bourgeois revolutions over the feudal system, which would place the action of the revolutionary party on the same terrain as capitalism, accurately assessing the problem, we must place the activity of the proletariat on the terrain of class conflict, which is the only way to spur capitalism to resolve by "its" own means the problems of "its" preservation.

Extra-capitalist areas can be found, for example, both in the Italian economy and in Russia. In these areas capitalism and its historical ruling class dominate, although it only controls a part of the economy, not necessarily the most important part.

The frontal attack against capitalism also involves attacking all remnants of the old regime, as both are in solidarity against the proletariat, thus solving indirectly, in a gradual development, the problem of reducing the extra-capitalist sector for the benefit of capitalism.

9. - *"Struggle to defeat the counter-revolution and push the Russian economy beyond feudalism and capitalism, a struggle that is conditioned by the mobilisation of the working class and the colonial peoples against white imperialism and the Asian lords."*

69

It is not clear if this struggle has to be considered as one of the current tasks of our party. To avoid any misunderstanding, we must clarify immediately that although this was, and should have been, one of the tasks of the class party until the Third Congress of the Communist International, to which we have no objection, today it is no longer true. We have to remember that Stalin's Russia is in fact the victorious Russia which came out of the Second World War, so it is at the forefront of current imperialist conflict to defend the fruits of that victory and, if possible, extend and consolidate them through a third world war, which is now in an advanced state of preparation.

The current line of conduct of our party regarding Stalinism and war should not give rise to any doubt. Given that this document is intended as a platform to be approved as a whole or rejected as a whole by the organisation, it should contain a call to clarify these problems which are so serious and ongoing. But we find that this document deliberately ignores the role of the Russian state in imperialism and war, and the tasks of the party on these issues. This gap, which is not an unintentional oversight, seems more serious because it has deeply muddied the consciousness of the party with theories of a capitalism "number one" and the definition of the Stalinist state as a state with peaceful interests and intentions compared with a warmongering North America.

IV. Party Activity in Italy and Abroad

3 - *"We are now in a period of depression and a revolutionary revival is out of the question for many years. The length of this period depends not only on the severity of the degenerative wave, but also the increasing concentration of enemy capitalist forces. "*

The term "out of the question" clearly contradicts Lenin's theory of the "sharp turns" characteristic of the imperialist phase. We agree with Lenin and are working so the party can become the driving force of any possible change.

"Sudden changes surprisingly quickly modify the social and political situation in an exceptionally sharp manner, which determine immediately and directly the conditions for action and therefore the tasks involved. Naturally I do not mean general and essential tasks, which do not change with historical twists if the fundamental relationships between classes remain unchanged. "(Lenin). The length of this period of depression not only depends on the severity of the degenerative wave, but rather on the intensity of the internal contradictions of capitalism and its drive towards rupture, which cannot be predicted by any scientific analysis or assessment .

7. - *"The party forbids the formulation or manufacture, in a free, individual manner, of alleged new schemes and explanations of the contemporary social world, it prohibits free individual analysis, criticism and foresight, even by the most cultured and intellectually*

competent of its adherents and defends the health of a theory that is not the result of blind faith, but the content of the science of the proletarian class, built of secular material, not thanks to the thought of men but to the strength of the material facts that are reflected in the historical consciousness of a revolutionary class that are crystallised in their party. "

This is a strange claim. It deletes with a stroke of the pen the opportunity to contribute to the development of a critical Marxism through study and militant activity of those who consider themselves part of the class, those who submit to the requirements, purpose and discipline of the class their ability to comprehend the laws that govern capitalist life from which they extract the reasons and the confirmation of the continuity of revolutionary theory. The theoretical elaborations of a Marxist worthy of the name are not personal, not abstracted from class reality, because in that case they would be outside the class and hence stop being Marxists. They act as an element of the class, or rather, express, as an individual, the collective feeling. Otherwise we could not explain why and for whom the editor of this and many other platforms has written, and continues to write, unless he deems himself, deterministically, as the sole repository of the correct interpretation of Marxism. In this case, this doctrine would become one of many "taboos" that genuine Marxism has taught us to despise.

8. - *"The party, although weak, does not relinquish its proselytising, trying to attract new members, nor does it give up the propagation of its principles in all forms, oral and written, although meetings have few participants and its press has a limited readership, since it considers that this is the main activity at this stage. "*

We must reject the claim that the press is the main activity at this stage; it leads us to directly confuse one of the instruments of the struggle with the struggle itself. Party policy is to develop activity with the class, in the class, an activity which revolutionaries carry out within their material means, including "the press", but not limited "only" to the press.

11. - *"Firmly convinced that the period of revival will be accompanied by the reappearance of massive economic and trade union associations, the party, while recognising that today it can only develop sporadic union work, never gives up on it, and when the numerical relationship between its members, supporters and the individuals organised in a given trade union unit is sufficient, assuming that this does not preclude the possibility of an autonomous class activity, the party will penetrate into it and try to win its leadership. "*

We have seen several versions or attempts to define the union problem, sometimes contradictory, from the same source. We take for good this latest version to assert that, although we agree to work in the unions because that is where a large majority of workers are to be found, and we also accept positions of responsibility on the Workplace Committees[60], taking into account the caveats and mitigating factors that are already known, we consider these organisms to be fortresses that have fallen into the hands of the class enemy and cannot be re-conquered from within in a peaceful and democratic way.

Existing unions, as well as other bodies of the counter-revolution. will fall under the blows of the revolutionary assault.

Meanwhile no one can predict whether the massive resumption of the workers' movement will bring about a true class union or other mass organisations that have already passed through the sieve of the past experiences of the workers' struggle. In the current situation, the centres of attraction and assembly of supporters and non-party elements are our factory groups, to which the party should pay the most attention.

12. - "Given the current balance of power and until future situations allow us to know if the capitalist state openly becomes the dictatorial form that Marxism considered it to be from the outset, eliminating elective parliamentary institutions, the party will not take interest in any type of democratic elections and will not operate on that terrain. "

We will not dwell on the tortuous nature of the argument which clearly demonstrates an unclear understanding of the electoral problem and reveals the concern, which we do not share, to prevent the party's participation in the electoral struggle in any situation. If we are serious about this strange and paradoxical way of stating the problem of abstention or participation, the party should not take interest in democratic elections simply because they are democratic, but would have to consider participating when the capitalist state, exercising its dictatorship 100%, abolished elected parliamentary institutions. This distinction between dictatorship and dictatorship, between Mussolini and De Gasperi[61], is really a rather poor way to argue categorically and absolutely in favour of a priori abstention.

We retake and reaffirm, without caveat, the traditional line of the Italian left from the Meeting of Imola (1920), through the Livorno Congress (1921), the Congress of Rome (1922) and the election campaigns of 1921 and 1924, which has always rejected the abstention principle, accepting the electoral method depending on the circumstances, on a case by case possible participation in the elections, and actually participating without any new element of a theoretical or practical significance leading the party to revise this particular, marginal aspect of its work.

13. - "Convinced that generations of revolutionaries quickly overtake each other and that the worship of men is the most dangerous aspect of opportunism, since, due to deterioration, with rare exceptions, it is natural that leaders of advanced age pass over to the enemy and conformist tendencies, the party pays more attention to youth and makes every effort to recruit and prepare them for future political activity, avoiding social climbing and deference as much as possible."

We consider both selection and evaluation of the human material of the party should leave out any assessment based on your birth certificate, which is likely to

The Debate with "Bordigism"

Crisis of Bordigism? Maybe, But Not a Crisis of the Italian Left

From *Prometeo* No. 4/5, 1953.

The habit has caught on, especially among the Communists of other countries, and we could add, through theoretical inertia, of confusing the Italian Left with Bordigism, or rather, with the name of Bordiga and with theoretical formulations that characterise his personal thinking.

It has come about because this comrade was always singled out due to the fact that no-one else experienced such adulation and so much "betrayal". In addition, his closest comrades were struck by his exceptional eloquence and theoretical elaboration, which stood out due to his wide knowledge and his gift of improvisation in the service of a technical, historical and philosophical education, which was wider than it was deep. We maintain that this prevented the comrades of the Left from acquiring a certain critical awareness and a continuity amongst themselves to form a solid core of struggle on an organisational level.

In the opposition to first Bolshevisation, and then Stalinism, Bordiga was submissive and inactive and took no initiative. From the Left's removal from the leadership[62] until the partial re-awakening of his interest which occurred recently due to pressure from the most conscious part of our party, Bordiga appears as the fighter who chose to remain for almost thirty years under the crushing defeat of the collapse of the Third International, which was accompanied historically by the consolidation of Stalinism in Russia and around the world.

The round of "isms" (Leninism, Trotskyism, Stalinism, Bordigism), which correspond to the phase of reflux of the great experiences of each epoch, the hallmark of this or that "Church" which the epigones of the doctrine, or virtuosi of any tactical innovation always make issue of, thus dividing it off in a process of decline, if not degeneration.

The recent decades in the history of the parties linked to the fate of the Comintern confirm this view, and there are few who escape this contamination, this ideology of withdrawal, to remain solidly wedded to key ideas rather than to the personal work or claims of the "masters".

Amongst these few are those of the Italian Left, who, being mostly in exile on French or Belgian territory, whilst others were imprisoned or confined on islands by fascism, were forced to openly distinguish themselves with the arbitrary and controversial name of "Bordigists".

The precise object of this study is to render unto Caesar what is Caesar's, and we will do so not only by appealing to a general objectivity which in reality is always partial and subjective, despite its good intentions, but also to the unbroken and documented experience of those years. If the parties of the International have emphasised Bordigism as a specific position, "original" in its thinking and tactics, more than ourselves, this is due to the controversial and "biased" interests of the governing bodies of the Comintern[63], which systematically sought to identify and confuse the Italian Left with the personal thinking and positions of Bordiga.

Nevertheless, we must recognise that four-fifths of the theoretical work of this current we owe to Bordiga, and at least until 1923, he always contributed four-fifths of the political and organisational activity of this current.

That said; we need to see when and how Bordiga's thinking really only expressed only his own views and, conversely, when one can say they have become part of the theoretical and tactical heritage of the Italian Left. That is to say, let's see how far Stalinism, both in Italy and internationally, has come to identify Bordiga with the Left.

But first of all, we have to assess the work of a militant of the revolutionary vanguard from the point of view of their contribution, however important, to general economic, historical and theoretical issues, or largely political and tactical practical problems. We believe that this must be done in the most impersonal way, even when it is very personal. It must be considered in the sense that, in whatever epoch a revolutionary makes their theoretical contribution, whatever their name, they can only develop this work through instruments they take from the pool of scientific work accumulated by the class. They merely take up the themes identified by their predecessors which taken to a certain level of development, correspond to a certain degree of maturity of the working class, under the impulse of the stimuli and needs at that given moment in the life of capitalism. Revolutionary intellectuals must get used to stripping their personalities of any vestige of 'culturalism'[64], the desire to put on themselves on a pedestal and gain personal success, following the bad habits of small town academics or cults like Freemasonry.

In this sense, owe to Marx another wise warning: that in the light of certain "Marxist" theories, Marx did not feel he was a Marxist.

We must sweep away once and for all that theoretical authoritarianism and that group mentality which makes one particular person infallible and the rest servile observers.

We wish to end this introduction with a statement, which for us is very important. The Italian Left took root in the fertile soil of a socialism tested by harsh, active experiences, full of lessons from the First World War. It embodied the revolutionary initiative of the first post-war period in continuity with a mature critical experience, and clarified its opposition, both explicitly and tacitly, against "Russian" guidance which was dominant in the Third International. It acted and still acts as a pole of attraction for the few residual forces still anchored to a class terrain and revolutionary struggle after the tragic dispersal of the unifying body which was the International, which passed bag and baggage over to imperialism and war.

And there are two ways to approach the formation of this left Marxist current, either by linking it to a political and theoretical consciousness related to the development of the events that led to the First World War, or to the analysis of this or that comrade or group. The former is a dialectical formulation consistent with Marxism, while the latter is a totally idealistic and subjective way to consider the role of individuals in the dynamics of class conflict.

The infancy of the Italian Left was characterised by abstentionism. A strange fate lay in wait for this fundamental idea; reality would subject it to harsh criticism and unexpected metamorphosis. This current was abstentionist, an abstentionism which operated on the theoretical and tactical terrain until the Livorno Congress (1921), from then until 1924, it agreed to participate in the elections with a more or less pronounced nostalgia for abstentionism.

This was a matter of surly and unpleasant polemics by the Stalinists, according to whom Bordiga had the tactical skill to compromise on the issue of abstention in return for the pittance which was party leadership. We would say that Bordiga never really developed the abstentionist theory in a structured and permanent fashion, so it was like one of those fruits which always remain a little bitter.

The poverty of of Bordiga's speech and the corresponding theses presented by the Italian delegation at the Second Congress of the International are notable for their negativity. They are only comparable to Lenin's arguments urging participation in elections and electioneering "tout court"[65]. In Italy there were many more urgent problems demanding solutions than this waste of time over a stale argument and the one-sided practice of abstentionism, which in itself did not mean that the revolutionary path was a substitute for the parliamentary path, a position as one-sided and obsolete as the position favouring participation in elections which ended up confusing revolutionary parliamentarism with things like the workers' government of Thuringia and Saxony. This represented a tragic end to the German and European revolutionary period and paved the way for Hitler.[66]

In this way we can clearly distinguish between the Italian Left on the one hand and

Bordiga and certain Bordigists on the other, the Left has never defended a theoretical, moral or constitutional abstentionism. It was not afraid to participate in elections, and when it did defend abstention, it did so as a simple tactical expedient, which is particularly useful in the phases in which the proletariat is carried away by the electoral illusion, an educational way to express opposition to all aspects of parliamentarism. Similarly, it has never accepted or endorsed that other aspect of Bordigism's participation in elections based on a purely quantitative and formal calculation. For the Left, what matters is the political struggle against the entire coalition of bourgeois parties, and not the number of votes that a movement like ours could obtain since, by its nature, it is destined to play no role in the field of bourgeois democracy.

In this respect, the Italian Left set out its precise theoretical and tactical features at the Imola meeting, when the Abstentionist Fraction was dissolved, and with even more precision in the fundamental theses of the constitution of the party at the Congresses of Livorno (1921) and Rome (1922).

Bordiga's ability when it came to clarifying the tasks of the party, another aspect which raised the passions of certain sectors of the Communist International, would be irrelevant if not for the fact that it represents an example of this comrade's ability to adapt and his theoretical instability, constantly ranging between his natural deterministic appreciation of the facts and a complacent dialectical evaluation taken from Marxism which he perceived and expressed in a deterministic manner, following the canons of positivist scientism, which he illegitimately employed.

So we can see that when the Italian Left disagrees with Bordiga, the origin of the disagreements is always in different ways of interpreting Marxism.

The policy developed by the party between the Livorno Congress and the Left's ejection in 1923, represented the political ideology of our current. It is not only still ninety percent valid, but is the only one that has survived and endured the ideological and organisational disaster that befell Lenin's International. The years 1924 and 1925 were a period of intense Bolshevisation of international parties, the changing of the leadership of the sections that were considered "infected" by leftism was the dramatic starting point. Opposition to this policy, which was secret in the Russian party, did not develop internationally, apart from the open complaint we made in creating the "The Committee of Entente". This was unprecedented in the history of the Italian Left. For the first time it's initiative took the form of a collective frontal assault by the rank and file, with Bordiga reluctantly being dragged along. This situation remained unchanged until the comrades of the Left were forced to take another initiative, to defend the theoretical contribution of Comrade Bordiga against Bordiga himself, now in voluntary retirement.

This bitter battle the Committee of Entente engaged in until the Lyon Congress

(1926) was a real and timely alarm sounded over a policy imposed by the central organs of the International, and requires further examination in the light of the developments that followed. Anyway, the fact is that in that historical situation there was no disagreement between the Committee of Entente comrades and Bordiga, but there was a tendency for this comrade to "weaken" in the face of the enormous pressure from Moscow, which considered this kind of pronouncement of the Italian Left as a break from the formal discipline they had implemented instead of true revolutionary discipline, as an example that might "influence" other countries, particularly the German Left.

During the Naples Meeting of the Left, where the Left had to decide whether or not to continue the work of the Committee of Entente, we should have proceeded as the majority wished, leaving Bordiga in a minority, in order to continue the fight until the Congress of Lyon, and not capitulate before, the then secretary of the International, Zinoviev's intimidation. Within a few months, the Left, which at the 1924 National Meeting[67] still controlled most of the party and had the solidarity and sympathy of the bureaucratic apparatus (at the time this term had not yet acquired the meaning it would later acquire in working class history), found itself alone in the desert. This is a phenomenon that deserves a separate chapter in the history of the Italian Left, but in any case it is certain that the more conscious comrades realised then for the first time the importance and seriousness of the fact that the life and future of our current were progressively dwindling in that largely fictional atmosphere in which Bordiga tended to isolate his thinking, living like a silkworm in the cocoon he had spun for himself.

It is very easy, and above all very comfortable, to attribute the dispersion of the Left to fascism, on the one hand and Stalinist reaction on the other. The fact is that from 1926 the Left virtually ceased to exist in the organisation of the Stalinist International, and all subsequent manifestations of this trend, both theoretical and organisational as well as its press, were developed without Bordiga. It based itself on a policy that largely diverged from his thinking and his "attitude."; an attitude that was not imposed by circumstance but of his choice, and lasted until the fall of fascism. Let us consider what is the origin of his isolation and how it relates to dealing with the ideological and political problems of Marxism. Bordiga never ceased to consider Russia as an economic reality dominated by its socialist character: for him, what had degenerated was the policy of Stalin and International.

From that moment, our positions diverged. As the Left continued to act on the traditional line based on a dialectical view of history in general and the proletarian struggle in particular, according to which the party and the duties of revolutionary activity are reduced to zero due to the change in objective circumstances, Bordiga as a consequence of his determinist way of thinking simply adapted to them. We said "consequence" without quibbling whether this conformism was used to justify his "doing nothing" or if it was the logical application of a personal iron-clad deterministic premise based on pulling in the oars on the boat and waiting for a radical disruption of the situation to be able to get back to talking about the Party and revolutionary activity.

Bordiga scrupulously adhered to this commandment without being involved for a moment either in the activity of the comrades organised as a fraction abroad or in the work developed by the first clandestine nuclei which revived the organisational ties which would lead to the formation of the party. And what is worse, huge events like the Spanish proletarian insurrection, the downfall of the International and World War II, waited in vain for his critical comment or theoretical collaboration, which might have demonstrated the continuity and strength of Marxist doctrine and might, above all, have prepared the necessary material in ideas and experience required for the future re-emergence of the class party.

We do not use this argument to focus the debate on an individual, but only to point out that the path of Bordigism differs from that of the Italian Left for the same reason that the dialectical method diverges from the deterministic method, because the revolution does not come about without human will.

His long absence from political struggle and formal and sentimental attachment to the Third International and the economic experience of Soviet Russia led Bordiga to a serious error of perspective: that is why he talked about deviation rather than counter-revolution; that is why he distinguished and classified capitalisms according to differing responsibility (capitalism number 1, capitalism number 2, etc..) instead of pointing out the role played by all imperialisms in favour of war, that is why he considered some of the contenders as progressive and others as regressive, rather than judge the war as universally capitalist and objectively counter-revolutionary.

In this way we, the Left, have come to the truly paradoxical situation of having to defend that part of Bordiga's thinking which is a legitimate part of the heritage of the Italian Left and reject what we believe does not correspond with Marxism and the interest of revolutionary struggle; in short, the Left has been forced to defend the best Bordiga against the Bordigism of the masonic lodge which has now begun to emerge. And out of all this we have been able to make out, especially because of the inconsistency and the surprising *souplesse*[68] that he demonstrated, what was the result of a particular mental vice and what was the result of genuine conviction or, to put it another way, what was due to his own thinking brain and what was intellectualist "taste" typical of he who replaces uninterrupted class activity with an easy use of the technique of paradox and a totally scholastic historicism, prone to see bourgeois forces carrying a "progressive" content in their midst, in a favourable light.

It is an undeniable fact that from the formation of the party until today, the differences we have discussed have gradually become more specific and clearer.

Although the militants of our party are aware of the problems that these differences have caused, which have had practical and organisational consequences, it is worth examining them again to see the differences and provide study material for an objective and conscious criticism of the Italian Left, which is too often confused with Bordiga or, even worse, with Bordigism.

Below is an accurate and irrefutable synthesis of the ideological and political nature of the Italian left:

1. - The dialectical interpretation of life and the world offered by Marxism has been confirmed by the vicissitudes of proletarian struggles as a valid and irreplaceable revolutionary theory and praxis. The permanent and concrete need is to establish indissoluble links between the party and the class, because the evidence shows that the party will become devoid of historical content if it is separated from the class, and the class would be lost without the guidance of the party, unable to fulfil its historic tasks relying only on its own strength.

The revolution, the exercise of the dictatorship, and the construction of socialist society are the result of the right combination of these two fundamental and interdependent subjective forces. Nothing happens in history without the intervention of human will, and that will would act in a vacuum if it were no longer the transforming element of the objective forces from which it is born and by which it is determined.

Amongst the subjective forces of the revolutionary movement, there is no determining factor that is not in itself determined.

The Left has managed to translate this theoretical guidance of Marxism, namely, that the bonds between the party and the proletarian masses, with their struggles and their interests have to be permanent. For the Left, even in the darkest reactionary periods, there are no objective conditions of the proletariat which necessitate the breaking of ties with the masses due to the fact that the latter might submit to the pressures of the enemy, and therefore may not constitute a historical class unity and may have definitely passed over to capitalism.

2 - Both in times of relative calm and during reactionary storms, the Left rejected the theory of temporarily taking a break until the capitalist world on its own produced a change in the objective situation. The historical process of capitalism's own internal mechanism would supposedly lead to an inevitable upheaval that would allow the revolutionaries who have taken a break to resume their place in revolutionary activity, which one fine day would resurface, almost miraculously, with new vigour ... This false and illegitimate anti-dialectical determinism, that does not take into account the ups and downs of the proletarian movement, which is unable to decipher even

in difficult situations what must be done but theorises only about preventing a loss of members, has never been part of the heritage of Marxists like Lenin. The October Revolution was not made possible by the sudden appearance of the Bolshevik Party, but because this party represented, for the masses moving towards insurrection, the culmination of decades of struggle, painful theoretical formation, contradictions and divisions, throughout which the confidence of the working masses never disappeared, even when they seemed absent, corrupt and dominated by the forces of counter-revolution and betrayal.

The Italian Left believes that the Russian experience lies completely within the framework of capitalism, with the particular feature that state economic planning, which originally was intended to build a socialist society, was the basis for the first and greatest experiment in state capitalism, an organic economic and political phase characteristic of the terminal phase of the development of monopoly capitalism.

The Italian Left believes that from an economic, social and political standpoint, the world capitalist mechanism, which is objectively a monolithic structure, is solid, even in countries where it appears less advanced and external signs of uneven development are more obvious. From this premise based on the most elementary Marxism and, given this basic character, perhaps it may not satisfy those whose theorising is more refined, we understand that the U.S. economy is exactly equivalent to the Soviet from the point of view of capitalist praxis, in the same way that American politics is exactly like Soviet politics as regards its class criminality, which lives on war and exploitation of the working masses of the entire world.

From Dialectics to Sophism

Since we have to clarify the way things really are, accepting or rejecting certain theories, we will say that Alfa's thought was always of interest in the Executive Committee (EC) in as much as it was an expression of a very distant world. All EC members were in agreement in saying that Alfa was stuck in 1921 and all his political judgments constantly expressed an intermediate ideological position between our party and Stalinism. The fact that today our opinion has changed about he who we can define as *"permanent secretary of triumphant opinions"* is something that does not concern us.

Let's get to the point, i.e. the clarification of the real disagreements that led our organisation to fracture, a split that the constant stubborn, formalist, sectarian attitude of Alfa made inevitable, since splitting the party in two freed him from the nightmare of walking in front of, or behind, the "donkeys".[69]

First disagreement: The way of conceiving the dialectic and the inversion of praxis. Second disagreement: The way of conceiving the dictatorship of the proletariat through the political surrogate of the party dictatorship.

Third disagreement: The class Party's attitude to Russia, when the Second Congress of our party had already resolved this definitely, also regarding the need for the party and the relations between the party and the masses.

And so we come to the latest findings, which systematised scientifically what previously had previously been presented timidly: on the one hand indifferentism, whose "ballistic"[70] potential exceeds that of nuclear energy and on the other hand that of a Marx and a Lenin as "supporters" of this or that bourgeois warring side in the wars of their times.

Firstly we must clarify that any comrade may have any opinion and sympathy they wish, provided they do not turn them into a theory and seek to impose it on the party.

What, today, should be the attitude of revolutionaries and the organisation in which they militate against imperialist war in general and its protagonists in particular?

If we walk, as we should, along the path of revolutionary defeatism toward the practical objectives of the revolutionary struggle, then it has no importance, or at most a mere abstract and intellectualist importance more appropriate to metaphysicians than to revolutionaries, to know which of the protagonists of WW3 will embody a "progressive" historical content and which is "regressive" and if, as far as the fate of the proletariat is concerned, we must desire the victory of one or another of the imperialist robbers.

We do not know what sense such desires have if the forces involved in their realisation do not act directly. That's for those to say, those who, like Alfa, reduce the dialectic to a boring game of abstract ideas and throughout World War Two played their role as leaders by insisting that their desire was to beat the Nazi-fascist regimes, while we had the audacity to ask the comrades if perhaps we would not have been wrong (fools, Alfa would say) to defend in different places, by other means and with other ideas, the revolutionary tradition of the Italian Left.

We are returning to this in order to clarify these ideas.

Once the era of national wars which could count on the help of the revolutionary forces came to an end, wars today occur between the contradictory forces of imperialism, and ultimately are directed against the working class of all countries.

The strategic problem that inspired both Marx and Engels (1848-1849) due to the prevailing pressure of the Tsarist Empire and the struggles for national independence, today no longer arises, Marx and Engels distinguished, rightly between counter-revolutionary peoples that served as the "Russian outpost" in Europe and the "revolutionary people", Germans, Poles and Magyars. In imperialist wars, the task of revolutionaries is not to join forces for the victory of the side that carries the banner of bourgeois progress on its bayonets, but to insert their struggle and the objectives of the class revolution in the midst of the vicissitudes of the bourgeois war. And calling a spade a spade, neither does the war in Soviet Russia, even if it were a defensive war, given its level of economic and social development, escape this iron law that presides over the entire structure of the bourgeois world.

In this regard, we will recall what we wrote in July 1946 (Prometheus 1, year I):

> "For Marxists, the capitalist forces that have entered the downward spiral of war to solve the problems of this or that imperialism, are not divided into opposing forces, one being progressive and another reactionary. Just as we have never shown sympathies or desires for a victory for the Axis forces, despite our critical analysis whereby we may consider that on the level of economic and political organisation, they are better adapted than the Anglo-Saxon to the current course of capitalism, tomorrow we will not show sympathy or desires that Soviet forces prevail when, for example, they fight against the Anglo-Saxon, just because the Soviet regime, i.e. the more advanced and characteristic regime of state capitalism, represents a historically more progressive stage of this economy evolving towards more vast and radical collective production and therefore closer to socialism and more impregnated by it. Capitalist development is based on its internal contradictions and not the likes and desires that its class enemies may profess. When imperialist war profoundly shakes the capitalist production system, including the laws that govern it, the essential and immediate task of the revolutionary party will be to act in accordance with the Marxist analysis of the nature of all imperialist wars, whose necessary theoretical justification is the development achieved by capitalism and its class antagonism, and not this or that other reason as the opportunists have a habit of stating, with great success. Given that the proletariat, albeit temporarily, could be crushed under the weight of the balance of power when this worsens, it remains a protagonist of history, it is up to the party to explain, to move it ever further away from the ideological influence of the war, revive it, direct it onto the terrain of understanding and class struggle, if possible channelling its forces to try to take advantage of an eventual favourable situation in which it can specifically raise the issue of transforming the imperialist war into social war."

This theoretical precision was inspired by Alfa's first revisionist signs with respect to the problem of the nature of war. While for us what was most important was the proletarian solution to the post-war crisis, Alfa hoped that the nation that had just arrived at capitalism might dismantle the citadel of capitalist preservation represented by a nation with a mature and solid capitalist economy. As if the force of a young victorious capitalism in this way strengthened a hundredfold would not be the starting point of a new cycle of exploitation of the proletariat and not push any possibility of socialist revolution further away.

Let us take inspiration from the classics. *"The other war (1870-1871) had accelerated development towards democracy, bourgeois progress: the fall of Napoleon III, unification of Germany. This war (1914-1916) can only accelerate the development of the socialist revolution."* Lenin, **Against the Current**.

*"In 1793 and 1848, both in France and in Germany and across Europe, the bourgeois-democratic revolution was **objectively** on the agenda [...] feudal and dynastic wars were then opposed objectively to democratic revolutionary wars, wars of national emancipation. Such was the content of the historical problems of the time. Currently, in major European advanced states, the **objective** situation is different. Leaving aside temporary setbacks, there is no progress if not towards a socialist society, towards socialist revolution. Objectively, from the point of view of progress, from the point of view of the most advanced class, bourgeois imperialist war can only be tackled by a war against the bourgeoisie, the war for power, without which there cannot be a step forward in a serious way."* Lenin, **Against the Current**.

"The war between England and Russia [referring to the threatening danger of 1885] in Afghanistan can bring the end of the bourgeois regime closer. But who do we wish will win? Who must be defeated? England or Russia? Guesde responds: I wish the defeat of both. And Guesde concludes whoever the regime to fall under the blows of the adversary, because we are dealing with different types of oppressive regimes, this is the gap through which the new social order can penetrate."
Whoever the imperialist giants may be, they are equally culpable, and their falling into the predatory war of 1914-1916 will open a breach through which the proletarian revolution will pass; that's how a Socialist must reason in our time.
"In the imperialist war of 1914-16 [in all present or future imperialist wars, we add] one cannot be consistently internationalist without being defeatist." Lenin and Zinoviev, **Against the Current**.

And defeatism is not about politically "supporting" anyone, not yesterday's Nazi-fascism nor today's Stalinist Russia, not even using the theoretical expedient which considers Soviet Russia as a country that the international proletariat should help in its struggle against feudalism.

Marx, Engels, and even Lenin were "supporters", and rightly so, of some of the national wars of their time, but it is obscene and ridiculous, on the eve of World War III, to try to imitate them by analysing the belligerents to know which of them holds the levers of further development of capitalism.

Have our disagreements come to an end? If it were so, nothing and no one could have prevented them from being resolved within the party.

The Irrational in the World of the Superstructure

Prometeo No. 19-20, first quarter of 1973.

How far can a misuse of language deform the thinking that reflects Marxist ideas and methodology? In assessing the role of irrationality in history, this is what happens when we question what is rational in human thought and action and, conversely, what is irrational. It is an ever present factor which sometimes dominates in the guise of a false appearance of rationality.

We are thus faced with a psychological, social and political problem which, to our knowledge, has not been given the importance it deserves in the extensive range of Marxist thought.

We do not intend to deal with this problem in depth but simply to raise the issue and critically examine what relevance it has, not just in theory, but also in political action.

This opportunity has arisen due to a critical, even if hesitantly formulated, comment by Giorgio Galli,[71]in his conscientious and intelligent review of my book dedicated to the complex personality of Bordiga,[72] published in *Critica Sociale* on February 5, 1972, No. 3, under the title: "PCI - Historiographic Alternatives."

Gallli puts it this way :

> *"It is true that, as Damen shows, Bordiga's position presents certain non-dialectical facets, an overestimation of rational action, which nevertheless is implicit in what Marx himself defined as "scientific socialism" within the framework of "historical materialism". But a dialectic that takes into account the dynamics of the world, which, as Damen himself says, "to a large extent obeys irrational impulses" is a dialectic that goes beyond what has been, until now, the conception of Marxism in its various interpretations, including the most revolutionary."*

The exact terms of my analysis discussed by Galli can be found here:

> *"Bordiga lacked a true evaluation of the dialectic because his education was largely based on scientific facts which led him to see the world and life on the level of rational development when the reality of social existence and of revolutionary struggle often put it in a world which was largely shaped by irrational impulses. The methodology based on mathematical certainties, which belongs to science, is not always in agreement with a methodology based on the dialectic which is movement and contradiction and this is no small matter when it comes to the analysis and perspectives of revolutionary politics".[73]*

From his remarks, it is clear that Galli has an implicitly materialist hypothesis, and thinks he sees in my formulation a hypothesis that could go beyond the formal dialectic, which does not see the constant relationship that must exist between the determining world and the world of the superstructure.

The first thing to clarify is that thinking that the dialectical relationship between cause and effect in any socio-political phenomenon is immediate is typical of an infantile materialism. In other words, that any given cause has an immediate and inevitable effect. Take for example, an objective situation of deep crisis in the system (as is the case today in the whole capitalist system), this must necessarily lead, according to a mechanical and automatic interpretation of the relationship with the superstructure, to a revolutionary solution, and with this in mind, we ought to prepare tactics and a strategy for revolutionary action that can count on the spontaneity of the masses.

This is the typical mindset of a political populism that pervades the self-proclaimed "left", from the extra-parliamentary left, whose myriad groups are too numerous to examine individually and too inconsistent for us to award them a decisive role in the crisis of the system, to the left and libertarian anarchist communist tendencies, or vulgar and messy Maoism. It is no coincidence that all these have flourished in a climate of imperialist domination, as elements that reflect the extreme paroxysm of its decomposition.

This mechanistic way of thinking about human affairs has always been very helpful to regimes in crisis, enabling them to catch their breath and buy time in the hope of patching up the fabric of their class privileges, against contrary laws of historical development. Does today's capitalism not come up against this contrary dynamic, deceiving itself that it can do violence to history?

We believe this outline of an argument deserves further examination.

In our time we certainly seem to have reached the highest degree of objective certainty in the domain of the natural sciences, both in its research and its discoveries. Science has achieved things far beyond what humans could have foreseen. Its technological revolution affects all our activities, sweeping away the remains of the past, acting as a profound force for modernisation that even affects the handicraft tradition, which in the course of centuries has accumulated an unrivalled potential of beauty and wealth. The development of the process itself acquires absolute rationalisation of production. These objective certainties, indisputable and universal, are within our reach, but humanity itself does not always have the awareness needed to recognise them.

Amongst these certainties we include the production process which, for good reason, is the most rational manifestation of the whole economy: indeed, it is impossible to conceive large industrial monopolistic complexes without strict planning, both concerning machines, raw materials and labour; calculated down to the last minute and penny, not to mention long-term development and profit. However, if we delve into the complexity of this process, it is not difficult to find the causes of vast and deep contradictions. For example, the constant growth of technology against the limits imposed by the market or the progressive reduction in the employment of labour power, and more particularly the fundamental contradiction between the increase, driven by competition, in fixed capital (machines) and the "global" trend of declining profit, which throws the scientific nature of the system into turmoil and causes such stress for the owners of the means of production. It is no coincidence that Marxism considers this mode of production as anarchic; it is unrealistic and contradictory, and therefore irrational.

But the argument is expanded enormously if we move onto the terrain of the socio-political phenomena of the superstructure, the terrain on which human beings think and act.

We are talking here about the dialectical relationship between determining factors and the superstructure expressed in class terms. More precisely, about two historic classes which at this stage are in dialectical contradiction with each other, during the long period of crisis leading from capitalism to socialism, from a society conditioned and based on the exploitation of man by man to one founded on freedom.

There is no doubt that capitalism has reached the final stage of its historical cycle, but not everyone is aware of the seriousness of the crisis that has overtaken this perfect but complicated and delicate production tool, or that science applied to technique has given to those who hold economic power, and especially the owners of financial capital, the power to become masters of imperialist policy. But if science applied to technique has developed the unbounded productive capacity of capitalism, it is now called upon to cure the ills that afflict the capitalist system of production and distribution. However, since science has found no better cure than ever more advanced technology to restructure businesses it gives only the illusion of a revival. All it reproduces are the same ills they are trying to cure only on a grander scale.

And of all these capitalist afflictions, the worst is that it is becoming less able to make a normal profit. Hence the pace of concentration of large industrial complexes has increased in the different branches of production: the big fish eats the small hoping to survive; leading to further polarisation between finance capital, in the hands of those who exploit all possible forms of speculation, and the rapid collapse of small and medium industries, since neither the state nor individuals want to take the risk of investing capital in companies with an uncertain future.

This profoundly complex economy, sometimes ridiculous, at other times tragic, faces the incurably unstable future of a dying capitalism. It continues to suffer in agony only because the weakness and errors of the class historically called upon to overthrow it, allow it to continue. The truth is that capitalism is not experiencing a crisis of growth, where it is structurally able to open up a new process of development, but the antagonistic class, the proletariat, has not yet become aware of its own goals and the revolutionary violence required to take it on and overthrow it. Capitalism does not die of exhaustion or because the bourgeoisie has completed its historical task; it can continue to live, as in fact it does, although it no longer has anything to give regarding the economy or social and cultural development. And this interregnum between capitalism, which can only exist under ahistorical parasitic forms, and a proletariat, still incapable of imposing its class hegemony, is reproduced in the superstructure, throwing all established values into turmoil and tending to return to a past that we thought had disappeared.

Since the current crisis has reached the depths of its disintegrating influence on production, i.e. the sector that better reflects objective certainty in relation to the coordinated action of science and rationalisation than any other, it should lead, in the realm of the superstructure, to a great many upheavals in the socio-political structures, exacerbating class conflict and awakening the revolutionary consciousness of the masses. If this has actually happened, it has only been partial, limited, if not completely deformed, demonstrating that the thesis to which we have referred above, according to which the phenomena of the economic base impacts instantly on the surface, in the minds of men, in their relationships and in their business, is absolutely inappropriate and invalid. In fact, the phenomena of the economic structure are projected onto the field of social and political relations in a way whose timing and location is difficult to assess, if only because of the different levels of development between individual capitalists' experiences, or because the process of rising human consciousness and will is slow and uneven, and depends on a unifying action, the first and indispensable condition for the instigation of a movement that may then impact on the determining base upon which depends the material realisation of historical events.

It is not difficult to compare the validity of these phenomena with real elements of economic, social and political development.

In other words, these economic collapses, even if sudden, are not always inevitably accompanied by revolutionary solutions if favourable subjective conditions do not exist for the class which is historically called on to carry out this act of revolutionary subversion. On the terrain on which the dialectical contradiction of social and political forces move, the problem of amalgamating collective consciousness to lead it towards a common goal is fraught with the greatest difficulties regarding its organisation, development, and solutions to problems that have been determined by the fundamental economic structure.

Taken as a whole, the working class is still bound more by a fictitious unity, of a sociological character, rather than welded to a political-economic basis. It is stratified and subdivided into different categories, and these in turn create contradictions in the world of work, in the degree of physical and mental exploitation and in the system of remuneration.

A class that thinks and acts in these categories is not yet a real class because it lacks awareness of its fundamental unity and its ultimate purpose. When it does act it obeys partial interests and immediate impulses as well as the union and political apparatuses that channel the mass movement into their parliamentary strategy, useful to both government and opposition parties. It is this background of irrationality which still pervades much of the working masses and the most irrational and perverse fact is they feel obliged to fight through increasingly feebler strikes and banal choreographed demonstrations not just for mistaken aims but even worse, aims that are against their own class interests.

The Tormented Maturation of Class Consciousness

In this vast and wide range of class elements, ranging from individuals to groups and categories which sometimes seem to be totally separated, actions, reactions and consciousness arising from the effect of the economic crisis that threatens the whole system become so distorted and contradictory that is not easy to evaluate them in a coherent way, not only as regards the economic and political but also, and especially, with respect to simple social psychology.

"The fact that you live and you may have an economic activity, that you procreate, that you make products, that you exchange them, determines a necessary objective concatenation of events, of development, a concatenation that is independent of your social consciousness, that can never comprehend it thoroughly. The higher goal of humanity is to comprehend this objective logic of economic evolution (development of social existence) in its main and general features, so that social awareness and the consciousness of the advanced classes of all capitalist countries adapt to it as clearly and distinctly as possible, with the most critical spirit." (Lenin)

All this should be understood not in the sense of a linear development, which would lead to idealistic or mystical interpretations, but a "contradictory whole" that shows the true, revolutionary sense of the dialectical movement of the process of development.

"This conception is the only way to explain this self-dynamic as it is, that gives us the key to the 'sharp turns', the 'solutions of continuity', the 'changes of direction', it is the only one which allows us to understand the destruction of the old and the birth of the new." (Lenin)

The proletariat is the only valid reference point in the dissolution of the traditional values of the culture in this phase of the bourgeois crisis; it is the historical bearer of the dialectic in concrete form. Engels regarded the German labour movement in the same way as the heir of German classical philosophy. In short, the modern proletariat appears as the only protagonist in this history, from the English industrial revolution to the current decadent and parasitic stage of the entire capitalist economy.

This explains why, in this historical period full of hard social and political struggles, this height of tension has not caused more than a diffused sense of agitation and revolt, with an indiscriminate use of violence, and why these agitations and revolts have failed in any case to take root in the deepest part of the class to express the basic essentials of irreconcilable class conflict.

This tormented maturation of a unitary class consciousness faces a long and difficult road and has not yet passed the stage of corporate, reformist demand movements in which the proletariat is still embroiled. The basic premise to attract workers back to the class struggle and revolutionary action is still missing.

Can the working masses achieve this by themselves? The advance of the industrial proletariat will achieve it, standing up for the entire class to the extent that they contribute to creating the conditions for the formation of a unifying, critical consciousness and a critique of the entire history of the labour movement, the fabric of the theoretical elaboration of the class revolution; of a body of doctrine that has matured in the fertile furrow of Marxism. These are conditions that presuppose the existence and formative work of the revolutionary party that will emerge at the right time out of the class itself.

It is for the party, and no one else, to assume the task of minimising the space between the rational and the irrational, which separates the working masses from the consciousness of what their class represents.

However it is not enough that the party has a valid framework, a solid doctrine and programme, if it does not have in mind these objectively pre-class areas which, as we have seen, are so vast and varied within the class itself and remain outside of its organisation. They have to be reduced when the time comes for active revolutionary practice.

If "*all social life is essentially practical*" and if "*all the mysteries that divert theory to mysticism are solved rationally by human practice and understanding this practice*" (Marx, **Theses on Feuerbach**), then the importance and urgency of the problem presented before the forces responsible for revolutionary action is clear, and consist of specifying and deepening the knowledge of the true nature of those grey areas that weigh on the class struggle and their possible and eventual use as "subsidiary" forces on the terrain of revolutionary strategy.

Axioms of Revolutionary Theory and Practice

Prometeo, No. 21/22 (First quarter 1974)

The nature and tasks of the revolutionary party is a problem covering a vast and turbulent area where the proletariat's struggle as capitalism's class enemy begins and unfolds.

But the fundamental interests of the proletariat are not always taken into account when addressing this problem and a positive contribution to the development of revolutionary theory has therefore not always been made.

In this analysis we aim to put together a factual, albeit limited, overview of the theoretical positions that we consider as the most characteristic of the Left spectrum, which is currently agitated by a plethora of self-styled "left" groups. These are hard to understand due to their improvised and superficial character. They sometimes make errors when, claiming to be objective, they approach the original sources of more qualified and responsible writers to use for their own ends.

It is not easy to bring order to the jumble of sometimes contradictory positions on the role of the party and the relationship between party and class, given the theoretical dysfunction that has affected most of the groups that claim to be of the revolutionary left, including the "Italian Left" considered as a whole.

Is the ideological and political theory (in which we believe and for which we fight) in crisis over the historical role of the revolutionary party, as conceived by the Bolsheviks at the time of Lenin and Trotsky?

Certainly not, but bear one thing in mind. Namely, that in the minds of many there has gradually been emerging a feeling of vague dissatisfaction and from there a certain impression of decline of the role of the party as a permanent working class body, as an indispensable factor for revolutionary action. This has happened for two reasons. The first is the end of the revolutionary wave and the counter-revolutionary transformation of Soviet Russia, which occurred without producing obvious class confrontation and violence but through an internal process of economic and social osmosis which is not easy to understand. The second being the banal identification of Leninism with Stalinism as if it was a historical continuation, in a different phase of the Bolshevik Party.

The "Italian Left" has to be credited with being the first to critically address the inherent problems regarding the party and their implications. We remain clear that the central point remains valid, and any deviations are the result of inaccurate statements on the one hand or due to the predominance of the subtle poison of a polemic inclined towards paradox, just to assert intellectual distinction, on the other. We will provide some specific references, by way of demonstration, going back more than fifty years of the specific history of the revolutionary party, in which the "Italian Left " was almost always an opposition current that had to overcome the enormous difficulties all revolutionary minorities encounter. The relationship between the party and class is dialectically linked, with both on the same level, i.e. placing special emphasis on neither the party nor on the class. We see the party as a part of the whole (the class). It is certainly the most aware, most prepared, most ideologically and politically willing, in short, the most advanced part of the class, which has the task of guiding and motivating the class itself. Speaking of the different phases that mark the historical process, Bordiga asks himself (in *Lenin – On the Path of Revolution*, 1924) [75]:

"What separates them? Between the State of the bourgeoisie and the proletariat there can only be the culmination of a revolutionary struggle in which the working class is guided by the communist political party, which achieves victory after demolishing the armed force of bourgeois power and establishes the new revolutionary power."

Repeating this argument, the same year in the journal *Prometeo* (# 4, 1924, *Communism and the National Question*): Bordiga wrote;

"In short, this interest is the interest of the proletarian revolution. That is, the interest of the proletariat considered as a world class endowed with unity and historical tasks, which tends to a revolutionary goal: the downfall of the bourgeois order. We can and must solve particular problems in terms of this overall goal.

The way to combine the individual solutions with this overall objective is realised in the fundamentals acquired by the Party, which are the mainstays of its programme and tactical methods. These fundamentals are not revealed immutable dogmas, but are themselves the results of the general and systematic examination of the situation of all human society in the current historical period in which we must take into account all the elements that emerge from our experience. We do not deny that this examination progresses continuously and the conclusions it reaches are progressively elaborated, but the truth is that we could not exist as a world Party if the historical experience through which the proletariat has already passed does not allow our criticism to build a programme and a set of rules of political behaviour. We could not exist without it, neither we as a Party nor the proletariat as a historical class with a doctrinal consciousness and a fighting organisation."

It is in these terms, devoid of any trace of intellectualism though we cannot prove it, that the "Left", through the hard work of building the Communist Party of Italy and its leadership became more perceptive and mature, and was able to express here through Bordiga the relationship which is not in any way formal, that should exist between the class party and the class itself.

In this regard, we reproduce here several formulations that seek to define the nature of the party and its tasks with regard to the class. They range from the *Communist Manifesto* (1848) to 1925 and, although they reflect different situations of class conflict, this does not diminish their value. First the extract from the *Communist Manifesto;*

> *Thereupon, the workers begin to form combinations (Trades' Unions) against the bourgeois; they club together in order to keep up the rate of wages; they found permanent associations in order to make provision beforehand for these occasional revolts ...*

> *Now and then the workers are victorious, but only for a time. The real fruit of their battles lies, not in the immediate result, but in the ever expanding union of the workers. This union is helped on by the improved means of communication that are created by modern industry, and that place the workers of different localities in contact with one another. It was just this contact that was needed to centralise the numerous local struggles, all of the same character, into one national struggle* [understood as a struggle extending over the entire territory of the State before going on to the international level] *between classes. But every class struggle is a political struggle. And that union, ... the modern proletariat, ... achieved in a few years.*

> *This organisation of the proletarians into a class, and, consequently into a political party, is continually being upset again by the competition between the workers themselves. But it ever rises up again, stronger, firmer, mightier. ...*

> *Further, as we have already seen, entire sections of the ruling class are, by the advance of industry, precipitated into the proletariat, or are at least threatened in their conditions of existence. These also supply the proletariat with fresh elements of enlightenment and progress.*

> *Finally, in times when the class struggle nears the decisive hour, the progress of dissolution going on within the ruling class, in fact within the whole range of old society, assumes such a violent, glaring character, that a small section of the ruling class cuts itself adrift, and joins the revolutionary class, the class that holds the future in its hands.*[76]

Extract from the Theses of the Second Congress of the C.I.

Extract from the thesis of the Second Congress of the Communist International on the tasks of the Communist Party in the Proletarian Revolution :

> *"The Party is only distinguished from the great mass of workers by the fact that it considers the historical mission of the working class as a whole and strives, along the*

way, not to defend the interests of any one group or trade, but the whole of the working class."

Extract from the Statutes of the Communist Party of Italy
Adopted unanimously at the founding Congress of Livorno:

"The indispensable organ for the revolutionary struggle of the proletariat is the class political party. The Communist Party, which brings together the most advanced and conscious part of the proletariat, unifies the efforts of the working masses, leading them from the struggles for particular interests and immediate gains to the struggle for the emancipation of the proletariat."

Extract from the "Points of the Left" of the Committee of Entente (1925)
These "Points of the Left", although a schematic first draft, do not say anything different from the previous well known fundamental texts :

"The Party is the body which unifies the outbursts of individuals and groups provoked by the class struggle . As such, Party organisations should put themselves above particular categories, and synthesise the various elements emanating from disparate categories of proletarians, peasants and deserters from the bourgeois class, etc."[77]

Extract from the Rome Theses (1922)

"1. – In its activity, the Communist Party, the political party of the working class, is a collective that works as a unified whole. The initial impulses that lead the elements and groups of this collective to organise for unified action are the immediate interests that economic conditions provoke within the working class. A key function of the Communist Party is the use of its accumulated energies to achieve objectives, which by being common to the entire working class, at the end of an entire series of struggles, go beyond, the interests of particular groups and the immediate demands that arise in the working class.
2. – The integration of all elementary impulses into unified action is manifested by two main factors: one of which is the critical consciousness from which the Party draws its **programme**, *the other is the will that is expressed through the disciplined, centralised organisation within which the Party acts. It would be wrong to consider these two factors, consciousness and will, as powers that can be obtained or claimed by individuals, since they are only obtained by integrating the activity of many individuals within a unitary collective body."*

In this historical sketch the definition of the party and the party-class relationship is unambiguous, but in the '20's it was expressed differently, i.e. in the brief interval from Livorno until the promulgation of the "Exceptional Laws"[78] which forced the party underground. These are the terms of a platform that was the unifying basis of the "Italian Left" and by which we have always been recognised. And it is on this supreme theoretical and political line that our party consolidated the pillars of the doctrine and political coherence of the revolutionary left.

If this is a theoretical constant that has characterised our current, we have to go back to a particularly significant article by Bordiga in which, it is true that he did not go so far as to question the essence of this theoretical constant, but he was able, by the way he expressed himself so absolutely, to give rise to erroneous, arbitrary and narrow interpretations of it, as in fact happened. We are talking here about the article *Party and Class Action*, in which we can already discern that contradictory theme that has accompanied the personality of Bordiga and has been so fruitful for the work of his usual followers, with whom Bordiga never had any luck. The article states:

> *"One can not speak of a class as a historical movement where there is no party that acts as the vanguard of this movement ...*
> *"The party is the indispensable organ of all class action; and therefore logically one cannot speak of true class action (i.e. beyond the limits of sectional interests or small immediate problems) where there is no party activity.*

This way of expressing himself, somewhat vague and deliberately abstruse, gives rise to various interpretations, thus opening up a road along which others could travel at will under the illusion of completing his thinking. Whether the conclusion contradicted the premise itself mattered little, as was the case of the "dictatorship of the proletariat". This inevitable historical outcome was converted, with a stroke of the pen, into the "dictatorship of the party".

This caution of expression is understandable, considering that we were in the years immediately after Livorno, when the "Left" administered and led the party, in which Bordiga had the greatest influence and responsibility.

It was not until the 1951 theses, written by a Bordiga now detached from any discipline of revolutionary activity, to see how this tendency to weaken the links between party and class was accentuated, with greater emphasis on the party than on the class.

> *"As the party* – he states – *alone and autonomously directs the struggle of the exploited class to bring down capitalism, it will also be the one to autonomously lead the state of the revolutionary proletariat."*

Is this not a clear denial of the validity to the dictatorship of the proletariat, as a class dictatorship exercised by the party to make way for the theory of a "dictatorship of the party" that in reality cannot substitute itself for the class as the historical antagonist of capitalism?

The class is forged historically, not just by acquiring a clear revolutionary consciousness of its revolutionary aim, but also throughout the preceding stage where precisely because of the party's critical work in trying to win over the working class, it gradually, slowly and painfully acquires its consciousness. Starting from mere corporatism and simple demand struggles, it becomes more united and mature in understanding its ideological, political and organisational role as a revolutionary class.

We have to go back to a small allusion made in the course of a dispute about "organic centralism", a formula that Bordiga considered the best interpretation of Lenin and the parties of the Third International's "democratic centralism", to understand this trend to authoritarian, ultimately extremely hierarchical relations, which lead to the worst Stalinism.

In the Leninist conception, the dictatorship of the proletariat is equivalent to the presence and continuity of class content based on democratic relationships in the context of strict centralisation of the dictatorship itself, hence the dialectical relationship between democracy and dictatorship. The fall of the State and the class dictatorship will open a period of the widest and most complete exercise of proletarian democracy, through which socialist society will be expressed and materially constructed.

This tendency to the total social involvement of the class, which is organised during the transitional stage in the very heart of the dictatorship, while foreshadowing the future as an active living factor, is part of the process of decline of the whole structure of authority, coercion and the exercise of power. This tendency is absent in a party dictatorship in which this dialectical relationship is, in fact, broken, to the extent that any decision is unilateral. Orders only come from above and revolutionary discipline is administered, even in the pre-revolutionary phase by, for example, Unique Commissars,[79] all for the sake of following a visceral anti-democratic passion. This leads, for example, to judging in a blinkered and police-like way, as if obeying personal ambitions, any contribution to theoretical development that seeks to deepen the critical understanding of particular phenomena originating from imperialist domination, that reflect capitalism in its advanced state of decomposition, using Marxist methods of research. Let us re-read paragraph 7 of Part IV of the "Fundamental Theses" (1951) edited by Bordiga:

"No movement can historically succeed without theoretical continuity, based on the experience of past struggles. Thus the party prohibits personal freedom to develop new systems or explanations of the contemporary social world: it prohibits individual freedom of analysis, critique and perspective, including the most intellectually competent militant, and defends the soundness of a theory that is not a product of blind faith, but the content of the science of the proletarian class, built with secular material that is not the result of men's thoughts, but of the strength of the material facts, which are reflected in the historical consciousness of a revolutionary class and crystallise in the Party."

Clearly, this leads us to discriminate between the chosen few whom divine providence enables to develop theory on the one hand, and the many individuals who unfortunately do not enjoy the favours of providence, and therefore are not free to try to critically clarify the course of events using Marxist method as a compass, on the other.

We must closely examine the effects produced by this way of conceiving Marxism which hides under a layer of varnish its inability to follow the complex dynamics of the working class, with its ups and downs and sometimes contradictory vicissitudes, in the slow process of forming a consciousness of itself, and which lead it to break the ties that bind it to the most immediate interests of daily life.

The "Absolutes" of Neo-Idealism

(Prometeo No. 23, second quarter 1975)*

This article follows the previous one (referring to it on the first line). Here Damen's main target is not Bordiga, nor even his International Communist Party, but the first split in "late Bordigism" which occurred even before Bordiga's death. Led by Jacques Camatte, the splitters formed the group Invariance in 1966. It took some of Bordiga's ambiguities to new and ridiculous extremes ending by denying the revolutionary role for the working class and ultimately excusing their own failings by the discovery that all political organisations were "rackets". We suggest readers glance at footnote 81 before reading this document (Translator's note).

Our critical examination of certain formulations in Bordiga's *invariance* (in *Prometeo* N° 21/22, 1974) on the nature, role and structure of the revolutionary party, did not arise from some nagging desire for controversy, but concerned the clarification of a problem, like the party, which is always open to debate and theoretical development. This is especially true when so many schools of thought, inspired by the outstanding contribution of Bordiga on this subject are involved in this debate, even if his contribution was sometimes contradictory. This frequent vivisection has ended up deforming and distorting what in Bordiga was but a simple intuition or fondness for paradoxes. We should remember here that Bordiga's usual response to our criticism of this way of approaching issues, which resulted in a distortion of Marxist method was that even a paradox may contain some element of truth, even if small and veiled. And he was right, but this intellectual "taste" could excuse, or rather offer a cover, as it has, to those who formulate theoretical speculations and look for any peg on which to hang their dissatisfaction and sometimes, their opportunism.

Our question is this: how far can we blame Bordiga, consciously or not, for having provided too many reasons for criticism for both comrades and opponents of the party? (Bordiga said he didn't give a damn and brazenly expressed a disturbing attitude with uncompromising brutality that made further explanation superfluous). This criticism has often been directed beyond the person of Bordiga to the entire "Italian Left" which has a very precise position in the international communist movement, rich in both ideas and potential.

It's not the first time that we have had to denounce one of the most heinous methods employed by the Communist International's bureaucracy, in which the bolshevised central organs of various communist parties immediately conformed in their fight against the opposition of the Left. This involved combating any current through a personal attack on one or other of its representatives, as happened with Bordiga himself. We had already struggled against these methods as a current in the Committee of Entente (1925).[80]

This kind of personal attack on individuals, and not against the complex forces that struggle on the class terrain, is totally anti-Marxist. If this initially motivated and consolidated our rebellion (in 1925 – translator), today it is even more reprehensible and must be rejected with contempt. Of course Bordiga, like anyone else, can be blamed for mistakes, indecision and personal rigidity which go beyond and against the very current which owes most of its theoretical contribution and development on an international level to Bordiga. But the communist left have to judge to what extent Bordiga's temperament and his way of putting things was responsible for this, and conversely, what in this complex debate became part of the heritage of the communist left in a thorough, inevitable selection process that flowed from the class struggle.

We have to recognise that, even when he was wrong, Bordiga always had a class perspective which envisaged the catastrophic end of the system through proletarian revolution. However the same cannot be said of all those who struggled alongside him, and who, in the name of a Bordigan "invariance", try to complete his work based on some of his inevitably incomplete theories, thus ending up outside Marxism. In the long history of the labour movement this is not new, but as a contemporary, even though marginal, phenomena we have to examine it. We mean here the tendency that has been called, with intellectual affectation, **Invariance,**[81] although it has actually ended up as anything but. We want to know how and when this current, which has grown under the tender care of Programma Comunista before subsequently coming out of it to take on a more Bordigist posture than Bordiga himself, began to work out its orientation based on the premise that Bordiga's work *"is only the starting point for further research that has not yet been developed."*

We just wonder, how is it possible that within an organisation[82] that claims to be from the Italian Left, which in the 60's included Bordiga, could produce elements and groups that, by replacing materialist dialectics and class revolution with a poorly digested humanism taken from Marx, argue that *"the communist revolution tends to affirm the human being, the true Gemeinwesen of man."*

The *Gemeinwesen* (community) is a leitmotif in the work of the young Marx and represents that point in human history where individuality begins to be overcome. Let us clarify this with Marx's own words:

> *"Exchange of human activity within production itself, and also of human products with each other is equivalent to … social activity and social enjoyment. Since human nature is the real Gemeinwesen of men they create and produce their Gemeinwesen, by their natural action; they produce their social being, which is no abstract universal power over and against specific individuals but the nature of each individual, his own activity, his own life , his own enjoyment and his own wealth. It emerges as an intermediary of the needs of individuals, i.e. it is a direct product of the activity of their existence. It is not dependent on man if this Gemeinwesen exists or not, but as long as*

man does not recognise himself as a man and has not organised the world in a human way, this Gemeinwesen appears in the form of alienation (Entfremdung) ..." (from Marx's notes to the work of James Mill)[83]

And in his *1844 Manuscripts*:
"Above all we must avoid postulating "society" again as an abstraction vis-à-vis the individual. The individual is the social being. *His manifestations of life – even if they may not appear in the direct form of communal manifestations of life carried out in association with others – are therefore an expression and confirmation of* social life. *Man's individual and species-life are not* different, *however much – and this is inevitable – the mode of existence of the individual is a more* particular *or more general mode of the life of the species, or the life of the species is a more* particular *or more general individual life."*[84]

These are brief, potted notes by Marx in which it is clear that several arguments run together with a tendency towards generalisation. They recall the Hegelian method Marx had not yet escaped from. This we know. But to refer today to the Marxism of the "*Manuscripts*" (1844) is to ignore the scientific Marxism of "*Capital*" and "historical materialism" and use the writings of the formative phase of the young Marx as a cover to promote one's own idealism.

The vision of a general and metaphysical return from the individual to the universal, that is, to this original and undifferentiated "community", the renewed *Gemeinwesen*, has more to do with Hegel's idealist dialectic than Marx's materialist dialectic. We find a clear manifestation of this method when examining the issue of how the revolutionary party was developed and what this meant in practical terms, which is central to our argument.

Below is a definition of the party, one of the last that Bordiga gave. It has resonated widely in the publications of this current:

"If the individual is in danger, and indeed this is no more than a lengthy period of wandering in the shadows that separates men from their history as a species, the way to combat it lies only in the qualitative universal unity of the party in which revolutionary concentration is achieved, beyond the limits of locality, nationality, employment status, the enterprise-prison of wage earners; it anticipates the future society without classes and exchange.

The party, which we are sure will resurface in a bright future, will consist of a vigorous minority of proletarians and anonymous revolutionaries who will have different functions, like the organs of a living being. However they will be linked from top to bottom through inflexible rules binding for all in respect of theory; by continuity and rigour in organisation; by a precise method of strategic action from which can be drawn a range of possible eventualities, all of which are subject to veto, based on the terrible historic lessons of the devastation wrought by opportunism.

In such a party, which at the end of the day is impersonal, no one can abuse power, precisely because of the inimitable characteristic that defines it, which follows a continuous thread whose origin lies in 1848. This feature is that the party and its members are not hesitant to affirm that their exclusive function is the conquest of political power and its centralised exercise without ever hiding this goal, until all capitalist parties and their petty bourgeois lackeys have been eliminated." (Excerpt from *Il Programma Comunista* n ° 22, 1958)

We do not believe it necessary to emphasise the universal character and mystical tendencies of this supposedly historic party that never existed except in the imagination of poets and the utopian aspirations of humanitarian pre-Marxist socialism. It will never exist, at least in the terms posed by Bordiga. Like us and sometimes more so, he suffered the anxiety, unmitigated by success, that arose from the difficulty of creating day by day, stone by stone, the first structures of the party which, the next day, would be dissolved by reaction and therefore had to be built again with other means and other human material, which are not always suited to the harsh discipline imposed by the construction of the party. So many difficulties and disappointments, including poisonous attacks from those who were comrades in name only, ready to surrender and more frequently to betray; that's the party we've known, the real party from Livorno to the Exceptional Laws[85], formed by heroes but also opportunists, full of sacrifices, prison, blood, but also corruption. Therefore, this is neither the time nor the place to make up stories about the perfect historic party; revolutionaries have always preferred to leave that to congenitally inept and visionary philosophers.

Bordiga had previously outlined that idea of the universal party, perfect in its structure and functions, as demanded by his mathematical mind and perhaps as a way to calm, with a perfectly idealist abstraction, the anxiety and dissatisfaction of a tormented life as a revolutionary. In practice, this idea of the perfect party served as a model to which the party should aspire and which was to inspire him to slowly and laboriously build an organ, the revolutionary party, composed of people with many differences, with the flaws and limits that entails.

But this tendency to abstraction offered possible sources of support to those who go in search of theoretical niceties such as "Invariance". This trend, which has emerged and developed within the latest phase of Bordigism leads the party at full speed into the unknown, the ideal model, the precursor of the future society. It writes thus:

"The party represents the future society. It is not defined by bureaucratic rules, but by its own being, and this being is its programme: it is the prefiguration of communist society of the free and conscious human species.

As a corollary the revolution is not an organisational problem. It depends on the programme. However it is obvious that the party form is the most suitable to represent the programme and defend it. And there are no organisational rules borrowed from bourgeois society, they derive from the vision of the future society. From this follows a major feature of the party. As the prefiguration of Man and of communist society, it is the intermediary of all knowledge for the proletariat, that is, for those who reject the bourgeois Gemeinwesen and accept that of the proletariat, struggling to impose it and therefore to impose the human being. The party's consciousness integrates that of all past centuries (religion, art, philosophy)."

And to end this triumphant and uplifting phase of the party that – allegedly – never disappears, we quote, again following *Invariance*, the last part of a letter from Marx to Freiligrath:

"I have tried to dispel that misconception according to which by "party" I understand a "League" which has already been dead for eight years, or a journal that disappeared twelve years ago. By "party" I understand the party in its broader historical sense."

This means (as explained immediately afterwards by *Invariance* with that finesse and logic that Marx lacked ...) as foreshadowing the future society, the future Man, the Human being that is the true human Gemeinwesen. The philosophy by which *Invariance* seeks to exalt the historical role of the party is based on the constant tiresome repetition of a phrase. In conclusion, it says:

"The continuity of our Being, the statement of our programme manifests itself both in periods of revolution and counterrevolution: the Party "in its broadest historical sense"."

It is a poor Marxist "historical sense" which ends up in the grip of a philosophy as old as it is opportunist and whose only value lies in the use, or rather abuse of capital letters! This brings us to the second and final phase of this current, which has led it to positions which are completely the opposite of its previous ones, mired as it is in a frenzied rush towards its own dissolution.

Is this some kind of political disease or is it simply a sign of inadequacy and confusion when trying to make sense of key ideas such as class, party, the dialectical relationship with the antagonistic class, etc... , which paradoxically becomes ever tenser until it snaps? Or is it more a matter of hangovers, of ideological and political frustrations that have particularly afflicted the younger generation of intellectuals with left Marxist tendencies that emerged from the Parisian events of May 1968? Probably a bit of both at the same time, and to see it gives us a pang of bitterness and regret, as this type of torment always leaves deep trauma, and also because, at the end of the day, the dispersal of young intellectual and human forces always weakens the revolutionary cause.

Now this pro-Bordigist experience has come to an end (in a fairly bad way it has to be said), this current has failed to draw the appropriate lessons. Instead it is submerged in events that are too large for its theoretical strength and seriousness and its political insignificance. This entire metamorphosis has occurred in less than a decade. Even in the May 1968 revolt *Invariance* took part randomly and was marginalised and it has not been able to extract from these events elements to strengthen itself, but only the grounds for its self-liquidation from ranks of revolutionaries who claim to be Marxist.

We Defend the Italian Left

Every so often we need to check our own political assumptions in order to critically evaluate our conduct in relation to what is currently going on. We also need to examine the behaviour of those who believe they are the repositories of who-knows-what coherence, with principles and methods that should be common to us all.

At first our aim was limited to a non-formal adherence to Marxist ideology and its correct application, without intending to carry out any restoration of this doctrine. However we found we had to distinguish ourselves from those who translate the thought of Marx and Lenin into idealistic, voluntarist terms as well as those who formulate it in terms of economism and mechanical determinism, following the precepts of positivism rather than revolutionary dialectics. The "Italian Left" has never endorsed the theoretical argument that says the party is **everything** and the proletarian masses **nothing**, precisely because this is based on an erroneous and sterile premise. This premise makes the party not just the advance guard and guide, something that we all agree with, but also sees it as carrying out the revolutionary rupture and exercising the power of the dictatorship, in the first phase of implementing socialism. In other words, not **with** the proletariat but **for** a proletariat which is unable to carry out this task for itself.

For comrades like that the October Revolution is a kind of a bastard, anti-feudal socialist revolution. It is socialist only insofar as it is based on the armed proletariat and a socialist programme. In short, they are talking about a revolution made only by the Bolshevik Party and not by an expression of the Russian proletariat.

But if we recognise the presence of the armed proletariat, it is precisely because the proletariat alone gives social content to revolution, and real substance to the work of its party. The fact that October is a socialist revolution is not just due to the Bolshevik party, it must be said clearly, but to the Russian proletariat, as a historically revolutionary class under the leadership of Lenin's party. It is clear that wherever the proletariat exists, whatever the extent and power of its development as a class, there is also a historical framework, capitalism, even if it is only a capitalist oasis scattered in the ocean of a backward and primarily agricultural economy. In spite of all this it is still capitalism, a capitalism that had already been the tragic protagonist of an imperialist policy in its first major conflict with the emerging Japanese capitalism, and had had its days of class terror when faced with the spectre of proletarian revolution, in 1905.

The Bolshevik Party had to take on an alliance of the Russian proletariat and the poor peasantry, which was possible then. It was a fortunate moment of a development that had, of necessity, to be Russian and international at the same time, as part of an international socialist revolution that had managed to break the chain of imperialism at its weakest link. There was a clear awareness that victory would not come about unless the Russian example was the first step in the international extension of the revolution. This would allow the development of socialist construction in Russia in line with a rising revolution in the major, more economically developed, European countries, such as England, Germany and France.

The Italian Left always based its fight on these principles, both within the Party and the Third International. Therefore, these recent theoretical contortions on the question of the party and the revolution are for us merely the amateurish exhibitionism of schoolchildren.

All this explains why, following the collapse of the Communist international, these comrades [86], who held posts of responsibility in the Party maintained that there was nothing further to be done for a whole historic period. So they retired to their tents substituting the tasks of revolutionary militancy, even at a personal level, with a facile intellectual coherence and an easy "sedentary" adhesion to the principles of the class struggle which though, continued without them, and against their very theories, first under fascism, then in the hybrid democracy which followed fascism.

It is precisely at the time of reflux of workers' struggles in Italy that these comrades adopted this mentality. They theorised the tactic of pulling in the oars of the boat, the dissolution of the party and a return to the tasks of the fraction, thus breaking up the one internationalist organisation that had proven itself in the fight against Stalinism. In whose interest?

For us the party is forged day by day through the slow and exhausting work of training cadres who cannot just be selected in periods of struggle or violent repression and disillusionment, especially when you are stabbed in the back by the betrayal of your own comrades.

It is not and never has been historically true that the party only emerges in a time of revolutionary assault. On the contrary, it has to be **militantly active** throughout an entire previous historical period before it can reach its fullness as an organ of leadership and revolutionary action.

In this regard, we must mention the ridiculous confusion that has befallen comrades when there have been spontaneous movements of the working masses, especially in the countries of the Soviet bloc. This confusion came to a head with the Hungarian events[87] which some, like the small group of exiles in France, have considered as a provocation of American capitalism. Others, however, have seen Russian armed intervention in defence of institutions and conquests that, while they were not Communist, were in any case progressive from the capitalist point of view, and therefore should be protected from Western capitalist attack. Finally still others have seen in these events a national anti-Russian front which supposedly includes the armed forces of the "workers' councils". The relativism that differentiates between one reactionary and another, between Thiers and Stalin, between Stalin and Khrushchev, between a reaction carried out by a parasitic capitalism and that of a progressive capitalism, leads to the same result.

Rather, this is an experience that must be sieved by a Marxist critique to delimit what are undoubtedly predominant, positive class aspects, and also point out the negatives. This separates us from those who seek to transfer to factory bodies which lack political tradition, a complete vision of the fundamental tasks of the class and especially organisational continuity and leadership tasks that belong to the party of the working class.

It has to be said, and we have already said it many times, that the "councils" really are the highest organic expression of the workers' struggle and their revolutionary consciousness, despite the fact that, in the absence of the class party, they can only go as far as insurrection, but not on to socialist revolution.

In short, we reject the conception of the party as an abstract entity that is not tied to the objective possibilities, that is not a living thing nor tested in the changing reality of the struggle. In short, one that does not translate the objectives of the revolutionary struggle into the terms of working class life. Such a party would just be an easy way out, a cultural circle functioning like Thespis' cart[88], in which one lectures whilst other comrades, reduced to the rank of mere cultural helots, nod in agreement.

No, this concept of a party is not that of Lenin who spent all his life among books, in struggle and exile, to prepare the human material without which the international proletariat might not have carried out those October days; if the Bolshevik Revolution is an undeniable historical fact, it is due to the fact that this party was tied to the working class, and the latter to this party, as an inseparable whole, in a time that had become objectively favourable to the revolutionary solution thanks to the collapse of one of the pillars of war and imperialism.

Is it not here, in these issues, that we can see what differentiates Blanquism and Leninism? Needless to say our place, the position of our party, has always been, and remains, on Lenin's side.

The Party

In line with the historical tradition of the class party, we have considered the problems inherent in its existence, convinced that in raising them we do not immediately solve them, but only make a start in doing so.

The main thing, therefore, is to address the central problem that has been, and is, the subject of our concerns, the existence of the party, or what is the same thing, its cadres, and how to adapt to tasks which change with the situation, whatever its numerical importance, its capacity for influence and the reach of its activity amongst the working masses in the anti-capitalist struggle.

The important thing is that we constantly confirm the precision of our ideas and our critique in events as they happen, monitoring closely the corruption that the class dialectic exercises on the body of those mass parties, which still claim to be socialist, and to help fight this corruption with a relentless and sharp Marxist critique. Above all, we also do this without tactical expedients or administrative solutions, i.e. without compromises, to bring towards the party those who prove to be ready to fight against capitalism and the parties that support it, starting from the premises formulated by Marx, Engels and Lenin.

In this sense, we do not share the mindset of those who will not get their hands dirty. We do not fear, we even seek dialogue with class elements who say they are interested in the problems of socialism and revolution and who want to engage in the hard work of rebuilding the party of the working class, and we are not particularly irritated or disgusted by those comrades who, having put an end to a long, sometimes too long, Stalinist experience have finally broken or intend to break with the party of Togliatti, provided they have a clear awareness of wanting to appropriate the ideology, tactics and discipline of the party of Lenin.

Basically, while in some ways the situation is different, today the same problems are again present, the same concerns about people and currents which emerged in the preparatory phase of the Imola Meeting[89] and the Congress of Livorno, out of which emerged the Communist Party of Italy.

There is no doubt that at that time the Abstentionist Fraction of the Socialist Party, given the impressive theoretical nature of its platform and effectiveness of its local groups at a national level, was the organisation that most actively opposed the political line of the party leadership and could now be considered, in embryo, as a party within the party. However, at the moment of the most acute crisis of the First World War, when the appeal of the experience of the first proletarian state which had emerged out of the October Revolution was strongest, Bordiga was fully aware that, though a specifically revolutionary party was needed the chances of success of the Abstentionist Fraction to become a party of the working class were limited. Although the split had taken place at the Congress of Bologna (1919), the Abstentionist Fraction, as such, could not objectively lead a party appropriate to the situation and the pressing tasks of the revolution. Given that the Abstentionist Fraction split had been possible at Bologna, not to have carried it out would have been a mistake of such proportions that would have forever compromised the theoretical orientation of the fraction, as well as its organisation and the name of its biggest promoter.

This was why Imola was a compromise meeting, a concrete anticipation of the Gramscian "historic bloc" of the left tendencies in the Socialist Party, in short, a centre where currents converged from diverse backgrounds, differing from each other on many issues, some critical. The Abstentionist Fraction was not really the focal point of convergence of these forces, even if it was its most important nucleus. The main focus was Lenin's ideas and the attraction of the October Revolution and the organisational needs of the Communist International.

Moreover, this did not contradict the Abstentionist Fraction's thinking but was in perfect harmony with its own decisions. In this connection we should remember the third part of the motion that concluded the National Conference of the Fraction in Florence (8 - 9 May, 1920), which mandated the Central Committee to

> "convene, *immediately after the International Congress, the Congress establishing the Communist Party, inviting all groups that fall within the field of the communist programme to adhere, both within and outside the Italian Socialist Party*".

But what happened was that soon after, at Imola and Livorno, this tactical policy was given a narrower theoretical-organisational interpretation.

These are the groups and currents which participated as equals in the Congress of Imola and formed the skeleton of the party at Livorno:

1) The already mentioned Abstentionist Fraction which deserves to be studied separately, given the positive factor it represented in this preparatory phase of the party and also given the negative factor of its eclecticism when it came to formulating and implementing its thesis on absententionism on the terrain of political activity. In the pre-Livorno phase, which was not very different from the current period, the essential problem was the formation of the revolutionary party and not abstentionism, and it was not historically possible to form this party on a programmatic basis in which the ideology of abstention had a predominant role.

2) The group L'Ordine Nuovo (The New Order). Given its social and especially intellectual composition, this group already anticipated a trend which would emerge later, giving a key role to intellectuals rather than workers, both in the factories and in the broader arena of revolutionary action. Influenced by the neo-idealism that prevailed at the time in the world of bourgeois culture, this group tended to Marxism, but a Marxism riddled with an idealism that contradicted the traditional schemes of socialism and the socialist left itself.

Indeed, while the Left Fraction thought that the revolution is subordinate to the existence of a party and tried to conquer its governing bodies to impart revolutionary will and leadership, continuing the traditional line of the class party, the Ordinovists thought less about the fundamental role of the party and focused their attention on the capitalist factory, regarding it as "the necessary form of working class political organisation, the 'territory' of workers' opposition." For these comrades, unlike the party and the union, the council

"does not develop arithmetically, but morphologically, and tends, in its most developed forms, to promote the proletarian conquest of the productive and exchange apparatus created by capitalism for its own benefit."

"The need for these new powers [the organisation of councils] to immediately flourish, irresistibly driving the great working masses, will cause a violent clash between the two classes in the course of which the proletarian dictatorship will prevail. If the foundations of the revolutionary process are not laid in the midst of proletarian life, the revolution will be reduced to a sterile voluntarist appeal."

The differences between these two currents focused on this idea: party and councils; the party has its historical setting in the territorial structure and political-administrative organs that capitalist development provides, while the councils embody the vital breath, the rhythm of progress of communist society. The highest form of consciousness of the proletariat condenses in the party, its doctrine and the theory of class revolution, whilst in the councils, worker solidarity

"is embodied even in the smallest details of industrial production, it is an organic whole, a homogeneous and compact system affirming its sovereignty, power and historical freedom."

We conclude, therefore, that these two currents, the most important in the Communist Party, had in common the perspective of the final outcome of revolutionary action, but they could not be further apart in terms of their original impulses, their methods, and even their understanding of Marxism: some professed orthodoxy and integrity, others were leaning towards syndicalist conceptions of the De Léonist kind[90], which even today attract workerist trends.

The circle of theoretical and tactical confusion of the groups that came together at the meeting of Imola was later expanded, if we take into account the minority currents and individual members, ranging from the Graziadei-Marabini[91] formation through the electoral maximalism of many actual or aspiring deputies, to young revolutionary combatants solidly anchored to revolutionary Marxism but not in any particular school or tendency.

We will have to come back to the experience of Imola when faced with the issue of rebuilding the party, since parliamentary opportunism, the corruption of those who sought to do well for themselves and the fact that opposing class interests predominated within the party ended up draining the struggle of its strength and clouded its aims after corrupting its ideological heritage. The reasons for the limits, shortcomings and contradictions that accompanied the formation of the Communist Party of Italy can only be understood by basing them on this critique.

Will these negative outcomes be avoided in the future?

Our view is that, rather than the organisational, statutory provisions and the dissolution of groups as such, we should stress the dissolution of their ideology, whenever they are alien to Marxism, to achieve unity not only in the purely formal organisational aspects (dissolution of groups, individual membership, candidatures, etc.), but also regarding the unconditional and comprehensive adhesion to a theoretical-practical platform from which emanates the conscious discipline that unites forces, gradually resolves the contradictions and ensures continuity of the revolutionary struggle. And so far we have been consistent to this critical orientation, which has been able to mature among us thanks to the experience we passed through during the formation of the Party at Livorno.

Centralised Party, Yes – Centralism Over the Party, No!

We should first address the issue of centralism which the "Programmists" have never been able to define in an "organic" way. Linked as it is to the interpretation of a given historical experience, it simply cannot be reduced to formal and scholastic abstractions.

These muddle-headed "left communists" argue thus: in Lenin's International, there were no "pure communist parties" so the use of the democratic mechanism was inextricably linked to what existed at that particular historical time. It is therefore obvious that an International unlike the Third, which consists of "pure communist parties", should be identified by a different internal mechanism and not by democratic centralism, which ceased to be operative with the death of Lenin. What happened after that, in the Stalinist era, is not covered in their analysis because it had nothing to do with the working class and the objectives of the revolution.

But to suppose, as the "Programmists" do, an organisation in a state of chemical purity, an international of "pure Communist parties" as opposed to that of Lenin made of "impure parties", is playing with a metaphysical paradox. Instead of formulating the problems of a whole series of historical events through the lenses of dialectical materialism, they adopt a formal mechanistic calculation, which tends to get lost in the fog of the most obsolete idealism.

We can tell these comrades in all certainty that there will be no international of pure communist parties, but only an international that will reflect within it the good and the evil, the contradictions and absurdity, of a society divided into classes, themselves torn by various layers of interest, social conditions, culture, etc. The assumption of communist parties in a pure state with an equally pure world organisation, even as a simple aspiration, is not the result of any serious investigation based on Marxism. It strangely resembles a certain mysticism which had its heyday in the twenty years of fascism.

Lenin's International certainly had its weaknesses, due to the immaturity of the historical period that followed the collapse of the Second International and the crisis then afflicting the capitalist world. Every proletarian organisation reproduces, though in a more advanced way, and on an inversely proportional scale, the characteristics of the historical period in which it was formed. And it is certain that the negative aspects present in the Third International will be present, although differently articulated in future international organisations, as amply proved by the objective conditions in which the various Left Communist groupings, who today claim the right to make a contribution to the reconstruction of the international proletarian party, are operating. Amongst these groups, the one that suffers most from intolerance and crises is the Bordigist "Communist Programme" where the dynamics of democratic centralism work more deeply, as seen in the explosive cycle of its internal contradictions. Today, for polemical convenience, the "Programmists" would like to pass off the Third International as made up of "impure" parties. But here's how Bordiga previously judged Lenin's International, in clear contradiction with the current positions.

> "After restoring proletarian theory, the practical work of the Third International towered over the divisions raised by opportunists of all countries in banning from the ranks of the world's vanguard all reformists, social democrats, and centrists of all types. This renewal took place in all the old parties and is the foundation of the new revolutionary party of the proletariat. Lenin guided with an iron hand the difficult task of dispelling all confusions and weaknesses."

The real strength of these Bordigists lies in their inconsistency!

How can this group, with its structure of an aristocratic and intellectual elite, with a filtered and distilled Marxism, developed in backrooms rather than in the storm of class struggle, contest the accuracy of what we are saying? So then, how can we resolve, with Leninist integrity, the debate over the two faces of centralism?

In the phase of imperialist domination and proletarian revolution no organisation of the revolutionary party can conceivably exist which is not based on a highly centralised structure. Perhaps this is the feature that most dramatically distinguishes it from parliamentary parties. If centralism is therefore an imperative requirement imposed by class conflict, the attributes of "democratic" and "organic" define the subjective terms of a polemical distinction that has never affected the substance of this centralisation. Who can say with absolute precision how far bodies involved in this centralisation make use of the tools of democracy (active participation and active control of the rank and file) and how far the centres of power are based on an authoritarian regime in the physical person of a leader, and through him, to the Central Committee?

For the Bordigists of "Programma" the problem is posed in terms that come from the counter-revolutionary practice of Stalinism. This is how they tried, finally, to clarify their extraordinary theory that goes under the name of "organic centralism". We have reproduced it above in the same words in which it was formulated.

But we need to clarify once and for all the relationship that has to exist between the centre and the base so that the party is structured and operates according to Leninist principles. An ongoing dialectical relationship exists between the members and the party centre. It is obviously on the basis of that relationship, in the context of theoretical and political platform already agreed that the party leadership develops its tactical action. Lenin never advocated, either in theory or in his political actions, any other way in which the organisation could act. And how can we understand the organisational formula of a Central Committee or of a leader who relies only on himself, on his capacity as related to a "set" of already planned possible moves (our emphasis) in relation to no less foreseen outcomes whilst the "so-called membership can usefully be ordered to perform actions indicated by the leadership?"

It simply means the same as the policy of the Central Committee under Stalin, once all working class elements had been eliminated from the dictatorship of the proletariat. It means a deep and irreparable rupture between the members of the party and its directing centre and the resulting slide into the open reconstruction of capitalism. It also means that the Central Committee of the Russian Communist Party and Stalin himself was tied to a "set" of possible moves that were perfectly planned in advance, that would be carried out with equal accuracy, in terms, and in a reality, we all know. What we are denouncing are the disastrous consequences which occur in a supposedly revolutionary party when its central organ, as a body, operates outside of the bounds and control of the organisation's membership.

But closer to our experience, we have to denounce precisely those who postulate, or allow to be postulated, this laughable distinction between a political membership required only to carry out acts indicated by the centre and a centre that is entrusted with such powers of foresight and divination that it does not offer us a very encouraging sight. And here we are dealing with comrades who in terms of preparation and long militancy are highly skilled and command the respect and confidence of the whole party.

Was the leadership of the Communist Party of Italy (PCd'I), through Bordiga's declarations to the Comintern, perhaps not bound to a set of possible options that denied the possibility of Fascism's rise to power at the very time when it was carrying out the March on Rome? And was this glaring error of perspective not "in correspondence with the no less foreseeable outcome" of jeopardising the party with the tactic of the offensive for the offensive's sake?

And who prepared a "scientific" analysis of the Russian economy defining the October Revolution as anti-feudal revolution after having celebrated it as a socialist? Had Bordiga not affirmed (in *Lenin nel cammino della rivoluzione [Lenin on the Path of Revolution]*): "The revolution will be made in Russia, by and for the working class itself"? And further: "Soviet power was victorious, the dictatorship of the proletariat predicted by Marx, made its tremendous entrance onto the stage of history"?

How should we judge someone who was the most prominent exponent of the party and of "left-wing communism" who refused to become a "militant" in the Internationalist Communist Party at the time of its formation, as he considered it a mistake to fight directly against "the national communist party" (the PCI)[92] with the excuse that the workers were in the party of Togliatti? Then, when our split occurred, agreed to enter the PCd'I provided that the rump remained true to him, politically neutered and reduced to a sect of parrots of not always digested formulae?

What was his contribution to the development of a critical examination of the nature of the Second World War and the role played by Russia as a major imperialist player, when he rejected our definition of state capitalism to speculate about Russia as a spurious form of "industrial state"?

There are many more questions but we have said enough to show how ill-founded, precarious and objectively dangerous is his claim to assign to the Central Committee and this or that person, whatever their esteem, or skills of divination, the tasks of arbitrarily developing our theory, and functions of leadership, outside of and above, the party as a whole.

Lenin, at his most personal and most decisive, by which we mean the Lenin of the "April Theses" had a desperate determination to "go to the sailors", beyond the formal organisation of the Bolshevik Party's Central Committee whose positions which were based on misunderstanding and compromise. Lenin was not operating on organic or even democratic centralism here, but acting as the chief pillar of the coming revolution, the only one who had understood and endorsed the demands of the working class and this is because his feet were firmly on a class terrain, because he thought and worked in class terms, and for the class, and had a very lively sense of history which teaches us that revolution loves action and hates cowards who turn up a day late.

In this constant dialectical relationship between the membership and leadership of the party, in this necessary integration of freedom and authority, lies the solution of a problem to which professional objectors have perhaps paid too much attention.

Any revolutionary party which is not a mere abstraction has to address the problems of the class struggle in a historical climate in which violence and unchallenged authority dominates. In order to increasingly become a living instrument of combat it can only be organised around the most iron unity. Its ranks therefore have to be closed against the general thrust of the counter-revolution. The revolutionary party does not ape bourgeois parties, but obeys the need to adapt its organisational structure to the objective condition of the revolutionary struggle.

The elementary tactical principle of the revolutionary party in action, is that it must take into account the characteristics of the terrain on which it works and that its members are adequately prepared for their tasks. We do not believe there needs to be disagreements on the question of centralism. These only begin when we talk in "democratic" or "organic" terms. The use, or worse, the abuse, of the term "organic" can lead to forms of authoritarian degeneration which break the dialectical relationship that must exist between the leadership and the members. The experience of Lenin is still valid, and it is vital to be able to fuse together, in a single vision, the seeming contradiction between "democratic" and "organic" centralism.

"Circles" and the Revolutionary Party

After clarifying the party's traditional thinking concerning the problem of centralism, a problem that sophists, pedants and obscurantists place at the centre of a debate that has neither head nor tail which reduces the question to a futile bar-room debate about whether centralism should be "democratic" or "organic", we think that centralism, understood and practiced by Lenin, is the best way to run a revolutionary party called upon to solve the onerous task of organisation and handling the most irrational and violent events, full of inexorable, unknown, unforeseen factors, namely, the revolutionary conquest of capitalist power, which is the most skilled and ruthless organiser of violence, whether police or military, that history has ever known.

But a revolutionary party, which for the most part should only be made up of worker cadres selected in the class struggle, can only be a powerful instrument of revolutionary action to the extent that its iron unity resolves the problem of permanent interdependence between the top and the bottom of the organisation, namely to the extent that the constant relationship between freedom and discipline lives and acts in the collective consciousness of the party.

And we come to another aspect of the debate that Programma started in such a clumsy and thoughtless manner: that of the "circles", in which today the chaotic and scattered anti-Stalinist left seems to be enclosed and almost lost. We use the adjective "anti-Stalinist" and not "revolutionary" because obviously not all anti-Stalinists are revolutionary, but only in certain cases. To what and whom do these circles refer? What are they really? What are the analogies with the historical phase in which circles were developed, with the period of the old *Iskra*?[93] Are there now objective conditions in place that allow these circles, assuming that they exist, to be a factor in the reconstruction of the revolutionary party, even if not a determinant factor?

It is always a pleasure, for its freshness and because there is always something new there, to look back to the events that preceded the Second Congress, in the years of preparation (1890 - 1900). The work of ideological, political and organisational delimitation of the different organisations which later went to make up the party had to be carried out then, following the plan drawn up by the old *Iskra*.

Lenin also thought it was the party's historical tendency that made (keep in mind that this happened two or three years before 1905, the year of the first revolution) the convergence of numerous groups so important, which although they did not have a common platform, did at least have a minimal agreement that could be used as an indispensable bond. This is how Lenin concretised the essential task of that Congress[94]:

"To create a true party founded on the ideological and organisational principles formulated and developed by Iskra. The three years of Iskra's activity and the fact of having been recognised by most of the committees, obliges the Congress to work in that direction."

"Iskra's programme and tendency should become the programme and the tendency of the party; Iskra's plans on organisational issues should be sanctioned in the party's organisational statutes. But it is clear that this will have to be fought for: the representation for Congress ensured the presence of organisations that had fought resolutely against Iskra (the Bund and Rabocheye D*yelo)*[95] *and others who, while recognising Iskra as the governing body, actually pursued their own plans and were distinguished by their instability in the realm of principles (the group "Youzhny Rabotchi"*[96] *and delegates of some committees who joined them). Under these conditions, Congress could only become the arena for the victory of the Iskra trend."*

And when addressing the challenge of unifying forces that were not homogeneous, following the plans of *Iskra*, Lenin knew he had to have the support of external groups as well as those representing *Iskra* itself, as the Second Congress was to make clear.

The debate, or rather, the altercation between all these tendencies arose over certain articles of the statutes, and not by chance. And this certainly did not happen because they posed a different way of solving apparently formal, purely organisational problems, but actually arose due to the political-ideological character of the statutes, intended to exclude, or rather, make it impossible to coexist in the same organisation, those forces perhaps seeking unity in good faith, but which did not conceive of, or want, the party as a concrete and irreplaceable instrument for the class and its revolutionary leadership.

Given that all this happened in the historical climate of the Second International where parliamentary democratic guidelines dominated, the commitment to legal struggle is not surprising, the strange thing is that we are still not clear that, as the experience of Lenin in the old *Iskra* shows, the solution to the party's organisational thesis involves having a political intuition deep enough to realise that the development of the revolution occurred in the context of an objectively conservative reality.

The clash between the militant activity of Lenin, and Plekhanov, Martov and Axelrod who were seeking a purely formal party unity (circles, according to them had "historical greatness", and had to continue to enjoy a permanent and active presence within the party), was because they expected that this delimitation of the party would act like a centrifugal force on the circles. Indeed, in the October Revolution, these forces would be on the other side of the class barricade.

The experience we went through in Italy is no less full of lessons, in the phase prior to the formation of the party. At both the Imola meeting, and the Congress of Livorno, overcoming the groups that could be defined generally as of the left provoked quite harsh and controversial internal disagreements, but the fact is that the agreement around unity developed with an ease inversely proportional to its sincerity.

It is true that what most contributed to make this possible was the attractiveness of the October Revolution, but one must take into account that, in Imola, no group played nor could play the role *Iskra* played in the Second Congress. Neither Ordinovists nor abstainers, nor pro-Communist maximalists ever claimed that "their programme and their tendency had to become the programme and tendency of the Party of Livorno". That is how far the domination of the politics of the Centre of the International extended.

What was missing in 1921 was a platform to serve as an effective central pole as did *Iskra* in the years 1890-1900.

The comic, yet at the same time sad, moment at the Congress came when the representative of the abstentionists solemnly declared the fraction dissolved and retracted its main demand, abstentionism, to allay the suspicions and ill-concealed anger of the maximalist representatives, expressed with eloquence by Luigi Salvatori during the proceedings. Another of the comic and pitiful moments at Imola was the sacrifice of *Ordinovism* on the altar of the party that was about to be born.

All this happened in a situation in which the real possibilities for revolution were increasing, but what would happen later when the reflux of the revolutionary wave led it to break on the wall of the counter-revolution? What would happen was what actually happened in 1924, when Gramsci and Togliatti grew their old horns back, namely, the original vices of immediatism and idealism upon which the experience of *L'Ordine Nuovo* in Turin was based. These were blunt weapons but, according to them, they were the most suitable for expressing the ideas and methods of the workers' struggle. They were the best suited to their changing conditions, when a policy of compromises and contingent commitments substituted the perspective of uninterrupted revolution and the catastrophic outcome of the class conflict; when, in short, it was time to be legalistic, in and in favour of the republican constitution, and all because with the apparent and transitory consolidation of capitalism it seemed that democracy was "untouchable" , i.e. not deteriorating over time nor was it subject to the changing and conflicting vicissitudes of capital.

In light of this double experience, we can now proceed to examine the current situation, in which the dispersion of the groups of the communist left is usually due to causes profoundly different to those we have discussed above, although the problem in the background is always the same, namely the rebuilding of a party capable of facing the demands of the revolutionary struggle.

But let's look at the true nature of these groups, paying more attention to their ideological-political features rather than their numbers. It is disconcerting to note that all claim that we need a party and all claim to be the party in embryo. In this sense, we can say that in the present situation in terms of the stature of men, their political foresight and sense of responsibility, the revolutionary minority is well below the experience of the old *Iskra* and even the Imola meeting.

If we cannot establish a criterion that differentiates the Communist left groups, then it would be impossible to justify and politically myopic not to consider objective factors which confer historical legitimacy on the theoretical elaboration of a sustained and consistent opposition to any policy of compromise and capitulation, as well as the building of an organisational base of selected cadres. We are part of the history of the workers' movement under the name of "communist left". The entire Internationalist Communist Party was born within this movement, having been the left opposition in the Socialist Party up until the Livorno Congress, the majority in the Communist Party of Italy until the Bolshevisation[97] of the party, after which it become the opposition until the outbreak of the Second World War. It organised itself as a Fraction in France and Belgium in 1928, in constant touch with the Internal Centre, which in 1945 resolved to organise itself as a party, following a class line which had never deviated nor broken through all these years, despite the twin attacks of the traditional class enemy and the new reactionary forces of Stalinism. And it is here, in a position where it has not always been easy to work but which nevertheless is always fertile, where one has to look for the ideas, motives, energies and experiences of new people, to get down to work resolutely on the enormous task of rebuilding the revolutionary party, with the prestige and moral and political authority this involves.

Besides the communist internationalists, who are responsible for this task not through natural or divine right or birthright, nor because they are deemed *primus inter pares*, there are other groups that have recently emerged from the crisis within the PCI, whose good faith or ability is not in question. But this is not enough to be a militant revolutionary, if one does not also prove capable of facing and successfully carrying out critical re-examination of one's political views in regard to the great problems such as the class nature of the Soviet state and the nature of its economic and political organisation, the nature of war in general and in particular colonial wars in the historic imperialist phase of financial capital. Finally you have to decide whether to accept the revolutionary strategy which means that in Russia, in China and in democratic countries directly or indirectly allied to these centres of power, the full extent of the problem of the conquest of power is raised. We have to destroy the structures of the capitalist commodity economy upon which the rising power of state capitalism is being erected.

The rise of these fractions can be attributed almost exclusively to the process of decomposition of the first workers' state, which has spawned a new opportunism which considers state capitalism in Russia as a phase required in the construction of socialism, or rather, as a necessary stage of the lower stage of socialism.

Those who do not take this into account will not understand what is common to the experience of Lenin's old *Iskra*, which unfolded in the historic setting of the Second International, and the current situation in which the historical problem of the revolutionary party is similarly up against huge barriers, sometimes insurmountable, on a proletarian terrain largely shaped by Stalinism which nurtures those bad mushrooms who call themselves Trotskyists, Bordigists or Maoists. They all claim to embody the ideology of the revolution, but actually diminish the political heritage of the entire proletariat to their own intellectual level, their own vanity, if not their own personal gain.

Therefore, these differences that separate the groups of the historical minority that claim to be internationalist are not insignificant from those who tend to merge into a single organisation and who generally originate from the chronic crisis of the PCI, although they declare themselves communist internationalists. The former recognise the need for a class break with PCI ideology and politics which have raged and still rage, in our country, while the latter, the Trotskyists, Maoists, pro-Chinese activists, must demonstrate with their theoretical contribution and political activity that they have broken all ties with opportunism.

And really in our analysis we are most interested in the former, the groups of the historical minority.

You Can't Build the Party Playing with Paradoxes

(from *Prometeo* 18 first half 1972)

A couple of words of clarification on the theoretical-political platform published by some French comrades based round the initiative *Parti de Classe*.[98] In line with the historic continuity of the "Italian Left" the formation of the Internationalist Communist Party in Italy represented the logical and necessary outcome of the Fraction. In the final phases of the Second World War the Fraction could not just re-form, faced as it was with new and more complex tasks that had to be addressed. In this line of continuity the Fraction was a passing moment between the party experience of the "Italian Left", the Party of Imola and Livorno with its final historical affirmation in the "Committee of Entente" (Comitato d'Intesa) through to its reconstruction as the Internationalist Communist Party (1943). This formed the only theoretical and organisational basis for any possibility of rebuilding the revolutionary party of the international proletariat.

Building the party in its traditional framework was possible in the historical phase of the collapse of fascism, which occurred concomitantly with a wider collapse, that of a socio-political and military front in the Second World War within which Fascist Italy was one of the most important pillars. The same operation would not have been possible at the time of the Fraction unless as a result of some slide into idealism and spontaneism and because the objective and subjective conditions necessary to generate its transformation into the party did not exist, not even in the slightest degree. Historically, the "Italian Left" was not and could not be, or embody, a "Belgian left" or a hypothetical "Franco-Belgian Left".

We don't need to cling to an indefensible thesis built on "*more geometrico*"[99] and formal logic to undertake a review of the events that led to the formation of the Internationalist Communist Party (PCInt). Sometimes, a mistaken theoretical premise, or at least one not based on Marxist methodology, does not lead to constructive criticism which, in itself, is always useful, but to its opposite: the slippery slope towards degeneration. Let's make the real issue clear.

The "Italian Left", despite the ups and downs of its experience, never had a theory that the party could only come into existence in a revolutionary period, and that it should dissolve itself and reduce its tasks to that of a fraction in a counter-revolutionary period. Was the Communist Party of Italy, created at Livorno under the ideological and political pressure of the "Italian Left", not founded in a period of growing counter-revolution? The experience of the Italian Communists during the Fascist period, with the shift of the party to underground work, is typical in this respect. In that period not only was the problem of continuity and contacting the masses solved, but also the training of new cadres, who could, of course, strengthen the Stalinist organisation[100], but proportionally, could also have been used to expand the area of influence of the "Italian Left". (In this connection it should be borne in mind that the expulsion of Damen, Fortichiari and Repossi from the party in 1933, was precisely because these comrades were working to rebuild the left fraction).

But a closer examination of the document reveals its most specious argument, and that is about the relationship between party and class. When it postulates that "the reconstruction of the proletariat as a class, that is, in a class political party" it is fully in line with a Marxist interpretation if it is saying that there can be no revolutionary class if it lacks a class party which come from within the class itself, but the postulate becomes a joke if it maintains that the party is useless when the class is temporarily a prisoner of opportunism and counter-revolutionary forces. This type of identity between party and class is undialectical. It is mechanically conceived and has all the seriousness and consistency of a purely intellectual exercise. The class as a whole, in its daily work and in the long history of its struggles has never gone beyond corporatist limits, beyond the stimulus of demands; trades union consciousness of the class has never become conscious of its historic goal as a revolutionary class: the battles, revolts, and insurrections which punctuate the long road of the workers' movement have rarely been transformed through their own virtues into moments of revolutionary assault of the entire proletariat against the capitalist system as a whole.

From here arises the historic, permanent function of the revolutionary class party which has to carry out the task of theoretical elaboration, preparation of cadres, and act as the scientific laboratory of the class to spur and guide the process towards the historic objective of seeing the proletariat constituted as the dominant class. To assign this task of self-sufficiency to the class in a pre-revolutionary period, as well as confining the building of the party to the period of the assault on power, where the consciousness of the masses is still mainly instinctive, even if its violence breaks the structures of the class enemy, means abandoning revolutionary Marxist methodology for metaphysical thinking. The latter replaces concrete, scientific data derived from economic and social reality with an ideological construct. And this brings us to the critical comments on the formation of the Internationalist Communist Party which are made by the comrades of *Parti de Classe*, which nevertheless refers to our experience (though it is appropriate) as something on which to draw out lessons and prospects for the construction, in their country, of the Internationalist Communist Party .

They write:

"Outside and against the erroneous and voluntarist attempt by Trotskyists to build a new international "born of the worst defeat", the Left showed that the duty of revolutionaries was not to attempt major practical tasks (which belong to revolutionary times), but to maintain the thread of continuity, not so much in organisational (in the narrowest

sense) as theoretical terms. But activism, an attitude then subjectively false in an objectively unfavourable situation imagines that the current situation can be changed not by objective economic factors (the end of the period of capitalist reconstruction), but through activity of a febrile character whose example would bring about a new revolutionary process. It is with this intention (despite some reservations) that in the midst of the democratic orgy (the intervention of the United States, the Anti-fascist Italian Committee of National Liberation) and despite the complete absence of the proletariat as a revolutionary class in 1943, that the Internationalist Communist Party of Italy, an artificial organisation whose practice we can say has always been inversely proportional to their theoretical effort, was proclaimed."

"At first, there was the illusion that the revolutionary party might not be ready in the immediate post-war situation because it was considered that the "war-revolution" schema where the victorious revolution of October 1917 was the outcome, would not fail, once again, to reproduce its essential lines in a militarily defeated, economically ruined, Fascist Italy. This schema could not be discounted since it was for this that the organisation was proclaimed - but because it did not try to gradually build itself: it had to be present and available immediately – this not only did not recur, we had exactly the opposite."

"The "party" of 1943, born not of the deep contradictions of capital, but of some surface wrinkles of its re-accumulation process in the period of reconstruction, gradually saw a reduction in the number of its militants, losing after 1948 all Marxist justification for its immediate existence."

Our Activism?

It's easy to see we are dealing here with an extremely hostile presentation in which it is obvious that adherence to certain positions typical of the "Italian Left", taken to the extremes of formalism can provide convenient cover for a deep but inarticulate critique of the Leninism that was and will continue to be the Leninism of the "Italian Left" which, in its most productive years and as a consequence of its activity, was total.

For the rest, there is also the *vexata quaestio*[101] (but not too much of the truth) of participation in elections and revolutionary parliamentarism which has also been prudently drowned out; that is to say, reduced to a tactical moment. This was badly understood by some epigones, subsequently won over by the left, who then brought to the fore the issue of the theoretical immutability of abstentionism. But even those positions have, in this specific case, a short life, and it is no surprise that the much vaunted "invariance" was ultimately reduced to a pile of shifting variations which piled ridicule on the more serious aspects of the inheritance of the "Italian left".

For us, the October Revolution is an undeniable fact that presupposes a Bolshevik party, that is to say that Lenin's party should be considered as a historical precedent and an ideal model to follow; everything else offered to us by the later revisionist, and objectively anti-Leninist, culture arises from the psychology of defeat of the revolution and is most often a by-product of a sentimental aversion to Stalinism.

We said that Lenin's party was the perfect model, the only successful one in the history of the revolutionary proletariat, and from which we draw the following:
The permanence and continuity of the party whose propaedeutic[102], and revolutionary work, is the stimulus without which the proletariat cannot release the handbrake and go beyond the limits of a trade unionist and corporatist consciousness that it naturally tends to.

It is necessary to retrace critically the positions taken by the "Italian left" even from the depths of the First World War to find the thread of its continuity, with the most significant steps being the Congress of Bologna (1920), the Congress of Livorno (1921), its leadership of the Communist Party of Italy until the dismissal of the left leaders (1923), and the Committee of Entente (Comitato d'Intesa) on the eve of the Congress of Lyon (1925-1926). The Fraction, made up of the traditional and most effective cadres of the Left, who had been the backbone of the Communist Party of Italy were then regrouped around the Committee of Entente to defend its majority political line against the leadership and its platform of opposition in the Congress of Lyons, against the new course imposed by the International. This fraction was therefore already a potential party.

In 1943, in the tumultuous and final phase of the Second World War, with the prospect of the collapse of a key sector of the war front, with the economic and political disintegration of fascism underway and the inevitable deterioration of the state structure, the basic and immediate task of the Communists was to work to create the most suitable tools for generating a favourable revolutionary outcome to the crisis. Lenin had acted in this way achieving a favourable outcome, but he would have acted in the same way even if the result was not consistent with the immediate needs of the party. Not one of those who believed then in the need for the organisation of the party was mechanically fixed on seeing a repetition of the events similar to those experienced by Lenin before the Bolshevik October.

The views expressed by Comrade Perrone[103] at the Turin Meeting (1946), which he later confirmed at the First Congress in Florence (1948), were open expressions of an entirely personal experience which contained perspectives based on a political fiction that it is not fair to refer if you want to make a valid criticism of the formation of the Internationalist Communist Party. Similarly, it is quite arbitrary and not based on any serious Marxist research to ascribe the later numerical decrease of the party to objective causes and to errors of perspective, while not having the courage to deepen their analysis of the internal process of disintegration which was the result of the defence of the personal interests of one who was not ready for militant activity, and disagreed over the analysis of the nature of the Soviet economy, and the role of Internationalist Communist Party.[104]

This is the climate in which we took on the initiative of building the class party, and any reference to Lenin and the Bolshevik Party was, and remains, the only possible and valid one in history. A different assessment would have been impossible because of the reluctance that was common to all of us to tie our work to a theory unrelated to the material situation of the class struggle, lost in the clouds of a theoretical paradox like, for example, considering the party and the historical legitimacy of its existence as mechanically linked to the reconstruction of the proletariat as a class. Hence the totally idealistic attempt to identify the party and class, as when the objective of the "reconstruction of the proletariat as a class, that is to say, in a class political party ..." is posed. This is intellectual sophistry that appears brilliant in its mathematical certainty, but is completely baseless when it relates to the vicissitudes of the class struggle and the historic and ongoing role of the party which is linked to the ups and downs of these struggles. In this aspect, the Bordigist distinction between "historical party" and "formal party" is no less false because there never has been a case of a party as the bearer of theses, doctrine, programme and capacity for development of revolutionary theory, which lives in the stratosphere and does not find every day in the heart of the class struggle, the reasons for the theoretical elaboration and constant confirmation of its validity.

The fundamental problem, and the most difficult to solve for a revolutionary minority is the problem of its presence and of operating on a political platform for a whole historical period of capitalism, whatever the objective conditions, including those of war and a counter-revolution still in progress, to help the working class to rise from a consciousness of its immediate interests to a consciousness of being the historical class antagonist to capitalism.

The problem of the continuity of the party is not our invention, but it is the characteristic position of the "Italian Left". Leaving aside what Bordiga notoriously wrote on this subject, we consider it useful to reproduce a significant passage from a statement prepared by the Executive Committee of the Left Fraction of the P.C.d'I in August 1933

> "With Fascism victorious in Germany, events took a different path to that of world revolution, taking instead the road that could lead to war. The party does not cease to exist even after the death of the International. The party does not die, it betrays. The party is directly related to the process of class struggle, and is expected to continue its action, even when the International is dead. Thus, in case of war, when the International has disappeared from the political scene, the party exists and calls the proletariat to take up arms, not to transform the imperialist war into a civil war but to continue its own

struggle even during the war ... ".(Excerpt from Towards the Two and Three Quarters International ...?)
Bilan, Year 1, No. 1).

We in the "Italian Left" who bear the responsibility for having formed the Internationalist Communist Party, even if we do not think we solved this problem, are nevertheless conscious of being in the process of working towards solving it. We have done this with perseverance, tenacity and through our ongoing contact with the factories, paying attention to the daily problems of workers in order to translate them into class terms, through issuing the party press which gives constant nourishment to activists on a national scale, and in the factory groups which we are in the process of building.

But we are not worried about knowing, with mathematical precision, where the task of the fraction finished and how and when that of the party begins. We lived through it all, we were the main instigators and we are proud to have done what we considered the right thing to do.

In this specific case, the Internationalist Communist Party has all its papers in good order: it has to its credit defined the capitalist nature of the Russian economy; openly denounced, in the middle of the Second World War, the imperialist role of Russia which is no different from the other belligerent States through its participation in the division of the world into spheres of economic and political influence; made a frontal attack on Stalinism as part of the global counter-revolution; struggled against the war and against the supporters of the anti-fascist national war movement, pointing out that it was in reality, a decisive factor in the strategy of U.S. imperialism and not an armed people's uprising against capitalism and imperialist war. Also to its credit, there is its open struggle, without tactical concessions, against the leadership of the Togliattian PCI, the Italian version of Stalinism. This poisoned the terrain of the working class forces emerging from the fascist war, already on the edge of being dragged into a new deception, that of the anti-fascist national war, a prelude to dragging the proletariat into the politics of economic reconstruction to resume the process of accumulation practically broken by the disastrous outcome of the war.

The Italian bourgeoisie owes above all (if not only) to the policy of Togliatti, and thus his party, the fact that the liquidation of fascism was largely limited to external appearances, and that the true essence of fascism, its nerve centres and essential structures passed safe and sound into the hands of the men and parties of the new Christian Democrat and Communist management, the two main pillars of the "resistance" and therefore the two biggest profiteers of the democratic-republican partyocracy.

Our party, strong in the best militants forged in the heat of ideological and political conflict at Imola and Livorno, or heirs of the Fraction; strong in the adhesion of large groups of partisans who had understood the real nature of partisanism, of whom everything could be asked except to lead the armed struggle in an anti-fascist rather than anti-capitalist direction; strong especially in the accession of young recruits committed to opposing imperialist war and the Stalinist mystification, forced the Togliatti leadership into a policy of provocations and blackmail to break and silence the only voice that at the time spoke in the language of the class and posed before the masses the only possible perspective for the proletariat, the socialist revolution.

The party's participation in the election campaign of 1948 has to be seen and understood in that context: it was not for electoral gains or even slavish application of the theses on revolutionary parliamentarism of the Second Congress of the International. There was only one goal at the bottom of the decision to be "participationists": inserting the party in the electoral mechanism was to enable the organisation to conduct a major battle of political clarification; not to ask for votes but to have the opportunity to show the working masses, in the broadest possible way, the true face of the revolutionary party which the press and propaganda of Togliatti's party sought to defile with accusations and insinuations that it always failed to prove. The occasion was more conducive than ever to face the beast in its very lair.[105] In reality, the party has never been offered, neither before nor after, the possibility to frontally and openly attack the Stalinist vulture in the factories, in the biggest industrial complexes, and on the streets, with the consequence of seeing the Stalinist front break every time and the alignment of the most politicised elements, and those most inclined to critical independence, with the internationalists. This tactic may seem adventurous only to those looking at the party with the fixed eyes of the Fraction.

In this regard, here is how the comrades of the "International Communist Left" expressed it

"Participation or not in elections is conditional and subject to the assumption that any tactic is justified only to the extent that, in any given situation, it helps to increase the political tension against capitalism." (From the *Draft Outline of the Declaration of Principles for the International Bureau of the International Communist Left*, 1946).

From a tactical point of view, the party was out in the open for the first time, and was engaged in the class war against the strongest and most dangerous fortress of the capitalist parliamentary democratic system.

Between a tactic which tends to bring the party out into the open and the opposite tactic of withdrawing from the game; between the development of the party and the reduction of the party to a fraction, we find the nub of the split of the party into two sections, which by a strange coincidence, then in fact became two parties. And what is worse in this review of the events is the discovery that the split occurred at a time in the history of the labour movement when the conditions were favourable for expansion and consolidation of the revolutionary party. This is demonstrated in fact by the continuity and the growing influence the two parties later had. It was the only political force in the Italian experience that embodied a tradition, a method, and a class platform of the revolutionary left which now has the task of patiently repairing the broken framework of internationalist unity. Moreover, disputes of theoretical, organisational and tactical issues, which had divided the two internationalist formations such as national revolutions, the nature of the Russian economy, the nature and role of the union in the imperialist epoch, are now behind us in the sense that two decades of experience have pushed the 1952 dissidents back to the original positions of the "Italian Left."

The Unions and Leninist Teaching

And we come now to the union question, the *punctum dolens*[106] of the minority of the French revolutionary left. The French group *Parti de Classe* to which we dedicate this note, start on this subject from a critical premise about the entryist tactic (it presupposes a different and opposing way of seeing the nature of the unions in the imperialist epoch) that we consider fair and which coincides with the position that our party has always supported, but it concludes with indications for tactics towards the unions that leave us surprised and greatly perplexed.

In this group too, the tendency to avoid the Leninist teaching on how Communists work with unions which are integrated into the system, is also alive. But to get away from the line drawn by Lenin's work involves, in every way, a vertical drop into the void. And it is somewhat surprising that a movement that claims to uphold Marxist methodology and is in the tradition of "Italian Left" addresses the union problem in terms of a certainty that is matched only by the simplicity of its formulation.

"*Tactically* - these comrades write - *the revolutionary party, instead of trying to vainly extend its influence in unions integrated into the capitalist system should instead exercise it in informal economic organisations that are created more or less spontaneously by workers – and even encourage – and transform them into vehicles of its slogans. Otherwise, this would introduce confusion among the workers and lead them to believe that the official union organisations belong to, or may be captured by them, provided a red leadership seizes them.*"

"*The mobilisation of the proletarian forces will no longer be in the official unions, but outside of them and against them.*"

The polemical argument that these comrades are conducting against the deformation of the policy on the unions as it has been understood and applied by the comrades of *Programma Comunista* and on which we agree, does not concern us because, contrary to the belief of the *Parti de Classe* comrades, we do not recognise that group, as the exclusive interpreter of the "Italian Left," tradition, unless you want to consider Comrade Bordiga as we knew him before and after Livorno, before and after the Second World War, as the personification of this current. In this case, the comrades of *Parti de Classe* are invited to send their critical analysis of the political line followed by the one section of the Left, ours, whose members were the initiators and organisers of the constitution of the "Committee of Intesa (Committee of Entente or Agreement)" (1925) which aimed to set in motion the defence of the current platform with an attack on opportunism; the same comrades who were the followers and leaders of the Fraction against its desired dissolution by Comrade Perrone when the Second World War broke out; those same members who, in 1933, were excluded and reported to the fascist police by the leaders of the PCI with the accusation that they were re-organising the "Left"; those same comrades who founded and developed the Internationalist Communist Party; finally, the very ones who, in order to defend the platform of the Left and its continuity, realised that they also had to break with the man who gave the Left, until 1926, the best of his theoretical and militant activity.

To return to the "union" problem, the best refutation consists in the reconstruction of the main points of what the party has done, and intends to do, consistent with the known position of the Left:

In the phase of imperialism and the planned economy, any planning would be impossible without the active consent of the unions. They have become in fact, on a par with the state and private entrepreneurs, guarantors of the success of the plan. The unions, having reached the top of the economic and political state of which they feel a necessary and integral part, the only policy open to them is to work with it, by subordinating the protests of the working masses to the requirements of its plans and the realisation of greater profits. It is only on this condition, which is offered by unions that have moved away from their historic task, that the plan is possible, and with it, the consolidation and the salvation of the system. But the union leaders can only do this if the unionised masses are ready to submit to their political power. This demands a strategy that limits and reduces the threat of intervention of the masses. This is done through the bait of the rolling strike always being offered to them, to deal with their wider and more pressing economic and political demands. From this changing reality, the union, whatever its politics, draws the sustenance that defines its existence and its functionality, throughout the entire history of capitalism.

If the union apparatus is integrated into the system, the mass of workers they oversee are not, or at least not directly, and they, however, have never stopped fighting against a capitalism which exploits them, although they are as yet unable to exceed the limits of trade unionist and sectional demands. This is basically the same framework experienced by Marx, by Lenin, by ourselves, and consequently the unions of the Third International have brought nothing new in relation to the Social Democratic unions of the Second International, or against the unions of today which bring such delight to our social and political life.

The mass of workers will not come spontaneously and autonomously to a consciousness of their essence as class antagonist. They will not come to the consciousness of the historical purpose that is implicit in their struggle against capitalism, but it is this same mass of workers who through their work create the objective conditions for that consciousness, and it is from this the consciousness that the class party brings together and elaborates the goal of the revolutionary propaedeutic[107] needed to revive the whole class. To this end the "Italian Left" aims to create with the permanent organisation of "factory groups", even in the midst of enormous difficulties, as training centres for ideological and political dissemination which become in fact vehicles for slogans critical of the unions. Factory groups solve the problem of contact with workers in the areas which are socially and politically the most sensitive to party propaganda, a prime and indispensable condition for a policy of recruiting new worker cadres on the basis of active militancy and revolutionary struggle.

Should we create a new union outside and against the official union? Or should we join new organisations arising spontaneously from working class initiative? Leaving aside the facile observation that new unions would never find enough space to form a self-sufficient grassroots organisation, even if it were possible, the new union would be modelled on the official union with all the faults and the few virtues of traditional unions.

We would like to ask the comrades of *Parti de Classe* to point out a single example of an unofficial union on an international scale which is an exception to our analysis and which can be taken as a model by revolutionary organisations, outside the experiences offered by the history of the workers' movement of the Second and Third Internationals.

If we then refer to the more or less spontaneously created union organisations which we might use to spread the union policy of the party, it must be said without fear of contradiction that those organisations which were formed on the wave of the union agitations of the hot autumn of 1969 by extra-parliamentary groups and students in Italy, France (1968) and elsewhere, have slowly faded away and are, in any case, forced to flow back into the channel for the maintenance of the system, bringing bitter and acute disillusionment to the few minorities who responded to their quite idealistic appeal. This is the reason for a new stampede to the parties against which they had carried out their so-called revolutionary struggle.

On the presence or absence of Internationalist Communists in the unions, let's look again at what is said in "*Draft Outline of the Declaration of Principles for the International Bureau of the International Communist Left*" (1946):

"A) In a historical situation where the problem of the seizure of power is not at issue, the mass organisation can only be based on demand struggles: the unions. When the situation becomes revolutionary, and the problem of the seizure of power is posed, it is then that we find the factory workers' councils (soviets), whose goal is not to advocate improvements in capitalist society, but to seize power in the factories."

"It is obvious that if the historical rupture does not lead to revolution, the process of the existing unions links with the state will continue. As long as this process is not over, that is to say is not completed, our position is to remain in the unions. If they remain statified then the question of giving birth to new mass organisations will arise."

There is one and only one fundamental problem which comes out of this debate: to break down the barriers of a theoretical premise vitiated by a series of fallacies which are linked by a formal logic, which ignore the actual and historic task of the workers' struggle and to distort it, by playing down the class role of the revolutionary party of the proletariat.

The assertion of the absence of the class in the context of the current situation is piece of sophistry, even if in class terms, it is temporarily defeated; and the consequences that is drawn from this is a fallacy which is that if there is no class there can be no class party genetically linked to it; and the final fallacy is the identification of the dictatorship of the proletariat with the dictatorship of the party by transferring to the post-revolutionary party-class identity from the pre-revolutionary period.

The conclusion? With a proletariat which is not yet a class, with a political organisation which is not a party, with official unions where workers are considered lost to the class struggle and to any attempt by the revolutionary minority to influence them ideologically and politically, the resulting framework, and the perspectives that can be drawn from it, would lead to our depressing self-elimination from the political scene if Marxism did not indicate that the following certainties, even if relative, are still certainties, permanently present in the labour movement.

The proletariat has been the only historically antagonistic class to capitalism throughout its existence. It comes to consciousness of its essence as a revolutionary class in the period of the attack on capitalist power, conditioned as it is by a process of education and development in the tormented and uninterrupted course of an irrepressible class struggle. This process of education and development is possible to the class because of the active presence of the party which is formed out of the class and engages with it in a powerful synthesis, the ideal reasons for its growth as a revolutionary force.

A Page from History

Bologna 1919:

The Congress that was afraid to say no to the International's policy of getting in as many as possible

[From *Prometeo* no.8, January-June 1966]

Today it is possible – we would say almost a duty – to make a retrospective, albeit one-sided, examination of the Bologna Congress (1919). We have to ask ourselves whether this Congress or part of it, certainly the most combative part, bears a huge responsibility for having delayed the formation of the party, an error which we believe still weighs on the proletarian movement.

A delay of only a few years (but which included unexpected and decisive turning points) meant that the Communist Party was formed at a time when the objective conditions for going on the revolutionary offensive had passed. The urgent need now was for a tactical commitment to defend the conquests of the proletariat from attacks by the forces of fascist reaction. This argument will be deepened when we examine the post-Livorno situation which was a time of mounting reaction. In the meantime, we will critically examine the problem of abstentionism which was the focus of debate at the Bologna Congress.

Abstentionism or anti-parliamentary electionism?

The debate on this issue is still open. Either you accept absolute abstentionism – which regards what came to be defined as the 'democratic' tradition of adjusting state or party policies according to the majority response, i.e. based on counting votes – as anachronistic, thus adhering to the principle of *a priori* abstentionism, an abstraction characteristic of anarchism and all those currents that see the world around them in idealist terms, or else you have to rely on the traditional positions of tactical abstention defended by Lenin and found in the programmatic theses of the Second Congress of the Third International.

The revolutionary party goes over to sabotaging elections when the proletariat is on the offensive and the prospect of the immediate conquest of power beckons. In this phase there is no place for the tactical use of the electoral system, and to act on such a terrain would eventually lead to the dispersal of the movement, always a dangerous thing and could lead to "constitutional" compromises such as those that divided the Bolshevik Party in Russia over the problem of power, and which in Germany resulted in the disastrous experience of the governments of Thuringia and Saxony.[108]

In a different phase of workers' struggle, when the objective conditions for the revolutionary conquest of power do not exist, Lenin and the International proposed parliamentary tactics as a secondary but inevitable expedient for the strategy of the workers' movement. Thus, the abstentionist tactic against any electoral participation and for boycotting parliament is valid in the crucial phase of class conflict, when the entire party organisation must not be diverted from the enormous offensive to conquer power. In all other cases, when faced with an electoral battle we have to assess whether or not to use the electoral system on a case by case basis. The abstentionists' mistake in Bologna was that instead of stressing the need for a split and forming the party, they focussed on abstention. This was the real error: the authentic militants of the fraction were fixated on the completely theoretical postulate of abstentionism, in itself useless as the basis for focussing on the goal of forming the class party.

Even so, there was no shortage of people who intended to make the abstentionist fraction the prime nucleus of the class party by objectively posing the problem of a split. Verdaro[109], well-versed in the problems of the workers' movement and a supporter of abstentionism, wrote in the preamble to the Theses for the Congress of Livorno:

> *The abstentionist fraction of the Italian Socialist Party therefore proposes to follow the process of its transformation into a party by implementing the split in the Socialist Party and founding the Italian Section of the Communist International.*

This statement was particularly significant because it clearly attributed to the fraction the following extremely pressing tasks: the cadres of the abstentionist fraction were to be the pole of the new party and bring about the split. These tasks had come about from the conviction that the Socialist Party could in no way be turned into a revolutionary party.

If the abstentionist fraction had really acted like this and presented itself as the centre of convergence and guide for revolutionaries during those very tumultuous years when the need to unite revolutionary forces was not always clear, the course of Italian history would have taken a quite different direction.

Given that the situation was incandescent, and on the edge of revolution, this tactic would have resulted in an infinitely more concrete and fruitful development than any participation in elections. However, an exaggerated loyalty to the fraction prevented a clear evaluation of the role of the revolutionary party, which gave their opponents the polemical pretext of comparing the abstentionist fraction to the Dutch "Tribunist" movement of Pannekoek and Gorter.[110]

Before and after Bologna it was impossible to be anything other than abstentionist and so you had to be oriented towards an authentically revolutionary policy. But who was going to carry out such a policy? What was the best way so long as the struggle was a function of the existence and preservation of the Socialist Party, a party dominated by the parliamentary group and torn inside by the irremediable conflict between the forces of reform and those of revolution?

If the abstentionist fraction had acted according to Verdaro's postulates, which at the time were shared by the entire fraction (i.e. first split and then the fraction goes on to form the nucleus of the new party) we can assume that this initiative would have taken place. Inevitably it would have led to the significant strengthing of the left, with non-abstentionists from Gramsci's "ordinovisti" together with those from the more general "maximalist" left!

The fact that such a glaring criticism can be made highlights the severity of the error. Bordiga, whose fault it was, himself also acknowledged this in one of his writings when he weakly comes up with the excuse that they were forced to compromise. This does not diminish but deepens his responsibility for the error, which is that had he proposed to the maximalists that they abandon their damaging abstentionism it would have resulted in the total castration of the fraction in exchange for the mess of pottage of the "excision" of the opportunist right (*Il Soviet*, 30.3.1919). The perspective was therefore to achieve a party without reformists rather than a new party built on the basis of the abstentionist fraction.

The Bologna Congress sanctioned neither perspective.

Why did the leaders of the abstentionist fraction fail in the tasks they had set themselves?

Who amongst the abstentionists has ever acknowledged that the perspective presented as the immediate goal was wrong, a perspective to which the entire fraction was theoretically committed? Apparently no-one. None of the members has ever addressed this problem; and from the thoroughly uncritical Bordigist publications themselves there is not much to learn in this regard.

Yet the objective situation posed the urgent need for a revolutionary leadership, and was particularly conducive to such an initiative. Potentially there were also significant numbers from the Socialist Party who were ready to join the undertaking. But no one dared to and, in the light of subsequent experience, it is possible to identify the reasons why they did not dare.

The basic error is always the same: namely, to see the problem above all from the standpoint of quantity. This is what led them to underestimate the role of the fraction from the point of view of its effectiveness and ability as an organisation; to minimise its influence amongst the masses and at the same time to exaggerate the consequences of electoral and parliamentary intoxication. In a word, the fear of failure, even if the masses were deeply motivated by the October Revolution, and the personalities of Lenin and Trotsky. Above all, there was a widespread belief that no serious revolutionary conquest could be made legally and by using the democratic parliament. All of this can be attributed to human frailty, to certain deficiencies of insight and revolutionary daring, but it does not explain everything.

The real reason, however, is to be found in the policy of the leading bodies of the Third International which, when confronted with the job of selection, of splits and regroupment, had adopted the tactical criteria of the maximum quantitative result and the least political discrimination, favouring, when not imposing, a split as far to the right as possible.

We know that in the face of such a political directive it was necessary either to passively accept or boldly break and leave the responsibility to others by going over to open opposition. In the specific case of the abstentionist fraction it would have meant breaking with the Socialist Party, cleverly emptied of its politically healthy elements, and promptly present the International with a *fait accompli* in order to force it to choose between the fraction, raised to the function of the party, as the only guarantee of the revolutionary struggle in our country, and the Socialist Party which would have completely failed in this historic task.

And when you do not act on this plan with the necessary decisiveness and speed, when you don't start to construct the party at the historical moment when it is most needed, or, when the party is formed – as in Livorno – it is too late, then it will have to lead a proletariat, not in an assault on power, but in full retreat.

Appendix One: The Fraction and Bordigism

The following short comment is taken from the Introduction to some articles by Onorato Damen on Ottorino Perrone (Vercesi)[111]republished in Prometeo 10 (March 1958)

The historical period in which the Fraction – as representative of the Italian left – began to test the validity of its tools of critical analysis, the accuracy of its theory and the merits of its programmatic positions, was when the experience of Stalinist Russia (we characterised Stalinism as "centrism" in those years) was already in advanced stage of putrefaction, and the Western world was smouldering in a crisis that would shortly lead humanity into the abyss of the Second World War. It was a particularly brutal time but the Italian Left did not confine itself to mere intellectual criticism, it goes without saying, but threw itself into the fire of political struggle. Above all it followed the continuity of thought that, in this period, better than in any other in the life of the Italian Left, was experienced and expressed in full independence of mind without any inferiority complex in the face of this or that personality. The absent Bordiga was kept in mind by publishing some of his old ideologically and politically more accurate and relevant documents, but his influence on those comrades was only through prestige.

Just as the events in the Spanish revolution were far superior to the participants, they also highlighted the strengths and weaknesses of our own tendency: the majority of *Bilan* appeared fixated on a theoretically impeccable formula which had the defect of remaining a mere abstraction; whilst the minority appeared on the other hand as being too concerned to go down the road to participation at any price, and were thus not always careful enough to avoid the traps of bourgeois Jacobinism, even when it became revolutionary.

When the proletariat goes on its revolutionary offensive, the solidarity, by which we mean active solidarity, of the revolutionary vanguard must not fail, regardless of the country in which the attack was triggered. Unquestionably the Spanish movement not only had a clear class origin, but was organised in a proletarian manner within the workers' own organisations and in the tradition of Bolshevik October.

The problem of active solidarity towards the Spanish proletariat posed a dilemma for our current. It had to avoid both an attempt to draw completely formal, scholastic and totally undialectical dividing lines between the phase of workers' initiative from below and that of its incorporation into the anti-Franco struggle of the Republican formations, as well as the need to avoid the illusion that this class initiative could continue in the POUM battalions which were certainly anti-fascist but were not always anti-capitalist. Since the objective possibilities existed there, our *Bilan* comrades had to pose the same problem, as arose when our party was faced with the partisan movement, by inviting the workers who fought in them not to fall into the trap of imperialist war.

In such cases, one must have in mind that any class initiative has to be measured by the degree to which it expresses a class content and what it achieves in terms of a class strategy. And when the objective conditions don't exist the implacable Marxist weapon of denunciation and criticism still remains, and this can be just as effective through intervention in events that take place beyond the class terrain. And this would have been the only way to avoid the split, and it should have been avoided, in the rare and irreplaceable fabric of our Fraction abroad.

Finally, we wish to highlight how some of the major problems of the revolutionary vanguard which we can realistically document were felt, and in a way which clearly expresses the continuity of thought and tactical vision of the Italian left, which passes through the Fraction, and became stronger and more mature in the experience of our party.

What did the Fraction state through the writings of Comrade Vercesi about the role of leaders? Here it is:

> *"Bordigism, reducing our movement to the person Bordiga, is the stupidest deformation in the opinion of comrade Bordiga himself who, following Marx, theoretically rejected any reference to the individual as such and proved that for the individual himself his only meaning can, and must be found, in the collectivity and in society."*

What did the Fraction state in the writings of Comrade Vercesi about the problem of revolutionary dialectic in relation to "economic automatism"?

Bordiga wrote:

> *"But Marxism has nothing to do with these gross distortions that would turn a historical science into economic and political alchemy in order to provide the philosopher's stone: the clash of economic interests automatically determines in every circumstance the ideology and role of social forces. While it is perfectly true that economic mechanisms push the classes directly down the road that leads either to their disappearance or their expansion, the dependence of classes in the production process follows an enormously complicated course.*
>
> *Classes, like all forms of social organisation appear, intertwine, develop, disappear, according to a law that immediately reflects the interests of the class that controls society, even one condemned by the evolution of the production mechanism. This "economic automatism" which diminishes Marxism can actually produce amazement at the "absurdity" of the situation in Italy and Germany where fascism was able to take power with the support of a part of the exploited masses while Marxism manages to understand these phenomena which, far from being "nonsense", are perfectly explained by the possibilities of political action and current political action, which may be exercised*

by a class that, like current capitalism is definitely condemned by the development of socialism."

And finally what does the Fraction state in the writings of Comrade Vercesi on the relationship between party and class?

"Today, after the experiences of the post-war period, it is clear that only a revolutionary party which is welded to the class by a system of principles, and a clear vision of reality, can represent the element that triggers the battle, pushing it in a historical direction prepared by all the antagonisms that have profoundly matured in the conflict between classes. Caught in the turmoil of events, without the party that would have prepared in advance the basis for action, the proletariat will only express vague aspirations, it will rise menacingly to collapse quickly, or it will be massacred by a ruthless capitalism ...

For Marxists, what matters is the evaluation of contradictions which ripen in social relations and in the struggle that heightens them, because it is in this way that the proletariat acquires the awareness of its own strength. Once detached from top to bottom from the structure of capitalism it throws the relations of production out of gear, but only on the condition that it is headed by a guide, a consciousness, a party."

And that is precisely what we have argued with Vercesi before, and also against Vercesi after.

These are, as we see, indisputable principles of the Italian left, which are always the indisputable principles in the daily struggle of our party, waged against those who, at some point, thought to turn their backs on this way of interpreting Marxism, which nevertheless is the only way to interpret it.

Appendix Two

A Brief History of the Italian Left

The first appearance of an organised Marxist left current in opposition to reformism took place at the Italian Socialist Party's (PSI) Milan Congress in 1910. A bitter confrontation developed around the Socialist Youth Federation which the Right saw as a "cultural" body whilst the Left saw it as school for revolutionary struggle.

In 1912, at the PSI's Congress of Reggio Emilia, the Left organised itself as the *Intransigent Revolutionary Fraction*. At the next Congress of Ancona the Communist Left defended the revolutionary programme against the Right whilst in Naples the Marxist socialists, with the young Amadeo Bordiga, founded the "*Karl Marx Revolutionary Socialist Circle*".

In 1914 the Parties of the Second International voted war credits for the imperialist war. The Italian Left were the only ones in the PSI to support revolutionary defeatism against both the interventionism of Mussolini, who left the Party, and the centrists who supported the ambiguous formula "Neither support, nor sabotage". The agreement of the Italian left with the positions of the International Left (at the conferences of Zimmerwald and Kienthal) was total. The key ones were "*fierce intransigence in the defence of the ideological borders of Marxism*" against the betrayal of Social Democracy, and for "*transforming the imperialist war into proletarian revolution*" (Lenin).

The October Revolution of 1917 was greeted by the Italian Left as the first act in the "*international social revolution*" and Bolshevism as a "*plant for every climate*". The Left defended all Lenin's theses against the Right and Centrist tendencies which dominated the PSI and in December 1917 founded their own journal "*Il Soviet*". It polemicised directly with the *Ordine Nuovo* group of Gramsci in Turin over the Factory Councils. The latter supported a position which was in some ways gradualist based on the identification of local bodies of a trades unionist character as the "*prefiguration of the future society*".

In 1919 the Left formed the Communist Abstentionist Fraction proclaiming its real theoretical basis in Marxism, in complete agreement with the tactical lines and strategic objectives of the Third International. The only disagreement was over the participation in elections and revolutionary parliamentarism supported by the Bolsheviks. At the Second Congress of the Communist International it made its contribution through a rigorous rooting out of opportunist elements (in the *Conditions of Admission to the International*).

The Italian Left as the Leadership of the Communist Party of Italy

At the Livorno Congress in January 1921 the Communist Left broke with the old reformist PSI. This was based on the "21 Points" of Moscow and founded the Communist Party of Italy, Section of the Third International (PCd'I), in which it held the leadership. Engaging in battle on all fronts – trade union, political and international – the Left openly fought both Social Democratic reformism and nascent Fascism. While for the Centrists Fascism was a feudal reaction, for the Left it was a political expression of capitalism in its attempt to confront its serious economic and social crisis.

However the isolation of the Soviet experience in Russia was now becoming clear. In the International, from the Third Congress on, we could see the first shifts to increasingly opportunist positions. This was the beginning of a series of expedients and elastic tactics which ended up by calling for a united front with other political forces alongside the ambiguous formula of a "workers' government", and finally to the counter-revolutionary idea of "building socialism in one country". With the PCd'I's own "Theses on Tactics" approved by its Rome Congress (1922) the Left had made a contribution, unique in the international field, to the solution of the most burning problems – from defining the nature of the party to the coherent practical application of communist strategy in the face of the evolution of bourgeois politics.

During the International's Enlarged Executives (up to the Sixth, in 1926), the voice of the Italian Left, represented by Bordiga, was the only voice to courageously denounce the seriousness of the situation that had been created in the Bolshevik Party and the International. In June 1923, the Italian left was excluded from the Executive Committee and therefore from the leadership of the PCd'I. A campaign of intimidation and censorship was implemented by the new Gramscian Centre imposed by Moscow against the representatives of the Left: from the suppression of the magazine "*Prometeo*" to the dissolution of sections of the Party controlled by the Left. It responded with the creation in 1925 of the Committee of Entente, which rang the first alarm bell against the degeneration of the Party. It was around this Committee that the most well-known and most effective leaders of the Italian Left gathered. Still the majority of the Party, they aimed to defend its political line when they had been the Party leadership and to support the platform of the Opposition to the new course set by the International. In May 1924, at the Como Conference, the Left still held a majority in the party. It was not until the Congress of Lyon (1926), where the Left presented its theses in opposition to those of the Centrists, that thanks to the manoeuvres of the new leadership who allocated all the votes of absent delegates to themselves, the marginalisation of the Left became official.

From Opposition to the Reorganisation of the Party

The Italian left who opposed the "Bolshevisation" of their own Party gave solidarity to Trotsky's opposition in the Russian party. From that time, Fascism and Stalinism unleashed their crackdown on activists of the Left, and forced most of the survivors to emigrate to France and Belgium. In 1927 the Italian left abroad met as a Fraction, and in 1928 at Pantin, it officially formed the Left Fraction of the Communist International (after 1935 becoming "Italian Fraction of the Communist Left") and published the magazines "*Prometeo*" and "*Bilan*". By following this red thread, which accompanied the interpretation, application and defence of revolutionary Marxism against the various renegades and class traitors, the Italian Left was able to form the Internationalist Communist Party (PCInt) in 1943, with the return from emigration of comrades of the Fraction abroad (along with other comrades, who had spent years in prison).

Thanks to the hard work of the Left, in following (and suffering from) the counter-revolutionary course in Russia and the International, the PCInt was defined right from the start by:
  - its unmasking of anti-fascism, including the alliance of the liberal-democratic bourgeoisie and the national-communists not to fight capitalism, but as an alliance with the national capitalists;
- the denial and rejection of the inter-class politics of the "peoples' alliances" and "united fronts" supported by Social Democrats, with Stalinists at their head;
- the rejection of any support for the forces of war and imperialism, whether Washington or Moscow;
- the struggle against Stalinism and any national road to socialism.

Today, when an uncontrollable and devastating economic crisis is shaking the foundations of the imperialist centres of East and West, communism is now on the historical agenda. This demands that the workers of the world organise and struggle in order to win their total liberation from the chains of capitalism.

And this can only be achieved through the destruction of bourgeois society and the overthrow of the capitalist system, which are both based on exploitation, oppression, poverty and are taking humanity back to barbarism.

Appendix Three
Letter of Bordiga to Karl Korsch[112]

Naples, 28 October 1926

Dear Comrade Korsch,

The problems we face today are so important that we should really be discussing them in detail face to face. This unfortunately is not possible at the moment. Also I won't be covering all the points in your platform in this letter, some of which could give rise to useful discussions between us.

For example I don't think your "way expressing yourself" about Russia is correct. We can't say that "the Russian revolution was a bourgeois revolution". The 1917 revolution was a proletarian revolution, even if generalising about the "tactical" lessons which can be derived from it is a mistake. The problem we are presented with now is this: What will become of the proletarian dictatorship in one country if revolutions don't follow elsewhere. There may be a counterrevolution, there may be an external intervention, or there may be a degenerative process in which case it would be a matter of uncovering the symptoms and reflexes within the communist party.

We can't simply say that Russia is a country where capitalism is expanding. The matter is much more complex; it is a question of new forms of class struggle, which have no historical precedents; it is a question of showing how the entire conception of the relations with the middle classes supported by the Stalinists is a renunciation of the communist programme. It would appear that you rule out the possibility of the Russian Communist Party engaging in any other politics than that which equates with the restoration of capitalism. This is tantamount to a justification of Stalin, or to support for the inadmissible politics of "giving up power". Rather it is necessary to say that a correct and class policy for Russia would have been possible if the whole of the "Leninist old guard" hadn't made a series of serious mistakes in international policy.

And then I have the impression - I restrict myself to vague impressions - that in your tactical formulations, even when they are acceptable, you place too much value on influences arising from the objective circumstances which may today appear to have swung to the left. You are aware that we, the Italian lefts, are often accused of not taking reality into account: this is not true. However, we do aim to construct a left line, keeping to a clear revolutionary strategy, valid for different phases and situations, but without ignoring their distinctive objective characteristics.

I come now to the subject of your tactics. Putting it bluntly rather than using ... official formulas, I would say that on the party's international relations they still seem too elastic and too ... Bolshevik to me. All the reasons you give to justify your attitude toward the Fischer[113] group, that is that you counted on pushing it to the left, or if it refused, to devalue it in the eyes of the workers, leaves me unconvinced, and it seems to me to have achieved nothing. In general I think that the priority today is not so much in the realm of organisation and manoeuvres, but in the elaboration of a political ideology; one of the international Left, based on the revealing experiences undergone in the Comintern. Failure here will mean that any international initiative is unlikely to succeed.

I am also enclosing some notes regarding our position on questions pertaining to the Russian Left. It is interesting that we see things differently: you who used to be highly suspicious of Trotsky have immediately subscribed to the programme of unconditional solidarity with the Russian opposition, betting on Trotsky rather than on Zinoviev (a preference I share).

Now that the Russian opposition has had to "submit", you talk of us having to make a declaration attacking it for having lowered the flag, something I wouldn't agree to do since we didn't believe in the first place that we should "merge" under the international flag unfurled by the Russian opposition.

Zinoviev and Trotsky are eminently realistic men, they understand that they will have to take a lot of punches before passing openly onto the offensive. We haven't yet arrived at the moment of definitive clarification, neither about the situation inside Russia nor about its foreign policy.

1. We share the Russian left's positions on the state political directives of the Russian Communist Party. We don't agree with the direction taken by the Central Committee, which has been backed by a majority within it. It will lead to the degeneration of the Russian party and the proletarian dictatorship, and away from the programme of revolutionary Marxism and Leninism. In the past we didn't object to the Russian Communist Party's state policy as long as it remained on terrain corresponding to the two documents, Lenin's speech on the Tax in Kind and Trotsky's report to the Fourth World Congress. We agree with Lenin's theses at the Second Congress.

2. The Russian Left's stance on the Comintern's tactics and politics, leaving aside the question of the past responsibility of many of its members, is inadequate. It is far removed from what we have been saying since the formation of the Communist International on the relationship between parties and masses, tactics and situation, between communist parties and other parties which allegedly represent the workers, on the evaluation of the alternating tendencies in bourgeois politics. They are closer to us, but not completely, on the question of the International's method of working and on the interpretation and functioning of international discipline and fractionism. Trotsky's positions on the German question of 1923 are satisfactory, as is his appraisal

of the present world situation. The same cannot be said of the rectification made by Zinoviev on the questions of the united front and the International Red Trade Unions, or on other points, which have occasional and contingent value and place no trust in a tactic that avoids past error.

3. Given the politics of pressure and provocation from the leaders of the International and from its sections, any organisation of national and international groups, which are against the rightist deviation, involves the perils of secessionism. We needn't aspire to a splitting of the parties and the International. Before a split is possible, we need to allow the experience of an artificial and mechanical discipline, with the resulting absurd practices, to run their course, never renouncing however our political and ideological positions or expressing solidarity with the prevailing line. The groups which subscribe to a completely traditional left ideology aren't able to solidarise unconditionally with the Russian opposition but neither can they condemn its recent submission; which didn't indicate a reconciliation but rather conditions under which the only other alternative would have been a split. The objective situation both in Russia and elsewhere is such that to be hounded out of the Comintern would mean having still less chance of modifying the course of the working-class struggle than by being inside the party.

4. A solidarity and community of political declarations would not in any case be admissible with elements like Fischer and co. who, in other parties as well as the German one, have had recent involvement within party leaderships of the right and centre, and whose passage to the opposition coincided with the impossibility of preserving a party leadership in agreement with the international centre, and with criticisms made by the International of their work. This would be incompatible with the task of defending the new method and course of international communist work, which has to succeed to that of parliamentary-bureaucratic type manoeuvring.

5. All means which don't exclude the right to remain in the party must be used to denounce the prevailing trend as one leading to opportunism and in contrast with faithfulness to the programmatic principles of the International, principles which other groups apart from ourselves also have the right to defend provided they set themselves the problem of seeking out the initial deficiencies – not theoretical, but tactical, organisational and disciplinary ones which have rendered the Third International still more susceptible to degenerative dangers.

I think one of the flaws of the current International is that it was "a bloc of oppositions" at local and national level. We must reflect on this, of course without indulging in hyperbole, but to treasure its lessons. Lenin prevented a lot of work of "spontaneous" development, counting on materially bringing diverse groups together, and only then fusing them into homogeneity in the heat of the Russian revolution. In large part, it did not succeed.

I understand that the work that I propose is not easy in the absence of organisational links, press opportunities, propaganda, etc. Despite this, I think we can wait. New external events will come and in any case I realise that the system of the *state of siege* will eventually exhaust itself, before we have to face provocations.

I think this time we should not get carried away by the fact that the Russian opposition has had to sign a few words directed against us, perhaps to avoid having to give in on other points in the tormented preparation of the document. Even these reflections enter into the calculations of the "bolshevisers".

I will try and send you items on Italian matters. We haven't accepted the declaration of war, which consists in the suspension of some leading left-wingers; the matter hasn't led to measures of a fractionist character. The batteries of discipline have fired into the wadding so far. It isn't a very satisfactory line and we aren't happy about it, but it is the least bad option possible. I'll send you a copy of our speech to the International.

In conclusion. I don't go along with your view that we should make an international declaration and neither do I believe it to be a practical possibility. What I do believe on the other hand is that it would be useful to issue in various countries declarations which have an ideological and politically parallel content regarding the Russian and Comintern questions, without though going to the extreme lengths of offering up a fractionist "conspiracy", with each fraction freely elaborating their own thoughts and experiences.

On this internal question, I subscribe to the tactic that more often than not it is best to let matters take their course, which certainly as regards "external" affairs is very dangerous and opportunistic. This is even more true within the special game of internal power relations and the mechanical discipline which I persist in believing is destined to break down of its own accord. I'm aware this is inadequate and not very clear. I hope you'll excuse me and in any case I extend to you my cordial greetings.

A. Bordiga

Appendix Four

Letter of Bordiga to Umberto Terracini[114]

Formia 4 March 1969

Dear Umberto

Your dear greeting for the start of this year has given me real joy and to be sure I agree enthusiastically with your wish for better times.

I follow the news of your activity and think, given the situation (that about Lenin was a reprimand for my benefit, but, I did not accuse anyone then, nor now) you are always acting for the better, just like forty years ago.

I remember loving your visit to Naples, I rejoice in all your old and solid friendship and I also thank you with all my heart.

I'm still waiting in my stubborn and sectarian position in which, as I have always foreseen our revolution will come by 1975; multi-national, and mono-partyist and mono-classist, or rather and above all, without the worst mouldy inter-classism: that of the so-called *student youth*.

For our part, when we had those green years, we did the best we could.

I am not returning to that stinking metropolis of Naples because I hope to bring about a cure in this better climate and to have some time yet to live, to repeat what I have defended in the past. My condition is getting better, that's for sure, and I see that my brain – certainly not electronic – can still be useful for something, not being at all abstemious from science, technology, philosophy and history.

I send you a warm and affectionate greeting with best wishes from me and my wife Antonietta, who makes enormous sacrifices to lavish care on me, even though, after so many years, she does not remember you, but rather Gramsci who, at my request, gave her some lessons in philosophy when she was young.

With affection, your Amadeo.

Allow me to draw your attention to my old article written in 1949, entitled "How we have always posed the question of *Intellectuals and Marxism*". It is reproduced in the recently released No. 4 of "*Il Programma Comunista*". I do not think you will find it in any parliamentary library. Anyway, it is on sale in Rome in the following booths: Piazza di Spagna; Piazza Cavour; Piazza Bologna; Piazza dei 500; Piazza Croce Rossa;

Via Carlo Felice; (San Giovanni) Cirioni Kiosk at University City. If that bothers you too much, I will send it to you if you ask.

Footnotes

(with section headings to indicate where they can be found)

Introducing Onorato Damen (pages 7 to 8)

[1] For a concise critique of Gramsci's positions see "Antonio Gramsci "Pre-Prison Writings":
Review Article" which can be found on the Internationalist Communist Tendency website at
http://www.leftcom.org/en/articles/2013-08-30/antonio-gramsci-pre-prison-writings-review-
article
Our next project is a translation of Damen's book "Gramsci: Between Marxism and Idealism".

[2] For a fuller account see the introduction to our pamphlet "Platform of the Committee of
Intesa 1925". See also footnote [9] below.

Amadeo Bordiga – Value and Limitations of an
Experience in the History of the Italian Left (pages 13 to 14)

[3] The Convegno (or Convention) of Imola (28 November 1920) was where the Abstentionist
Fraction of Bordiga's communist current united with the Turin group of Ordine Nuovo in
deciding to put forward at the next Congress of the Italian Socialist Party [PSI]at Livorno
a motion accepting the decisions taken at the Second Congress of the Third [Communist]
International. The rejection of this motion by the PSI led to the foundation of the "Communist
Party of Italy, Section of the Third International" [PCd'I].

[4] Enrico Berlinguer was, like Gramsci from the island of Sardinia. He was leader of the
Italian Communist Party [PCI] from 1972 until his death in 1984. Under him the PCI,
in a failed bid to get into power, adopted "Eurocommunism" and distanced the party from
Moscow, especially after the Soviet invasion of Afghanistan. The "historic compromise"
describes his failed attempts to seek a rapprochement with business leaders and other capitalist
parties. Gramsci was claimed as the inspirer for these policies by both Berlinguer himself and
many others both inside and outside Italy. See footnote [11] below for more details.

Introductory Note to the First Edition (1971) (pages 15 to 16)

[5] The beginning of the formation of the Internationalist Communist Party in Italy dates
back to the end of 1942 and took concrete form in 1943 when many of the comrades from
the Fraction abroad gathered around Onorato Damen and Bruno Maffi. Its newspapers at the
time were initially the clandestine *Prometeo* and *Battaglia Comunista*. In addition to the attacks
of the fascists, the Internationalist Communists endured those of PCI: they are not only verbal,
with defamatory accusations ("spies of the Gestapo") and continual provocations, but also with
physical violence that led, in 1945, to the assassination of two comrades, Mario Acquaviva
and Fausto Atti. The clandestine *Prometeo* was defined by the Stalinists as "... a filthy sheet

diffused by the police and where the rot against revolutionary melts and merges with espionage and provocation, with the Ovra and Gestapo which this leaf has become the instrument "(*La nostra lotta*, organ of the PCI). The PCI encouraged workers to "beat up" (the expression is from the PCI newspaper *La Fabbrica*) internationalist militants who are active in the strikes of 1943 in Asti, Casale Monferrato, Turin, Milan and Sesto San Giovanni, where in some cases they suffered deportation to Germany. (See the booklet: *The internationalists' confrontation with Stalinism, and its victims* [Prometeo Publishing]).

Introductory Note to the Second Edition (1977) (pages 16 to 19)

[6] The Third Congress of the Communist Party of Italy (PCd'I), which was held in exile in Lyon (1926), sanctioned the dismissal of the Left current from all governing bodies. The Directorate, with Gramsci to his head, *"Lyon made sure that the Bordigist far left is represented in a measure that did not match the strength it still had in the party"* (Berti "The first ten years in the life of the PCI, p.188). Bordiga made the same comment ("History of the Communist Left" in *Programma Comunista* No. 12, 1961): *"... All activity became clandestine, the idea of the centrist party leaders was very elegant: it was decreed that all the Membership cards which did not appear to vote either for the centre or the left were to be counted as being in favour of the theses of the centre."* And the centre obtained 90.1% of the votes of the Congress, given the absence of most of the delegates of the Left, who were monitored in Italy by the fascist police, with passports suspended by order of the Ministry of Italian Interior. The Left was thus marginalised and the party was totally dominated by the new ruling group, aligned with the political schemes of Moscow, which now put the all-powerful General Secretariat in charge of the party.

[7] "Gruppettari" - In the 60s and 70s, a series of far-left "groups" blossomed, which were mainly located outside parliament (the so-called "extra-parliamentary"), whose activists were sometimes called "gruppettari", frequently in an ironic and derogatory sense.

[8] Karl Korsch, German philosopher and communist, had broken with the Communist Party of Germany (KPD) in 1926 from a leftwing point of view, because he criticised its domination by Stalinist . On this subject see the book by Danilo Montaldi "Korsch and the Italian Communists", Savelli, 1976. This publication contains the letter Bordiga wrote to Korsch which we reproduce in full for the first time in English in Appendix Three.

[9] The Comitato d'Intesa (variously translated as Committee of Entente, Agreement or Understanding) was formed by the comrades of the Left (with Damen, Fortichiari, Repossi, Vercesi, Lanfranchi, Grossi and Venegoni) in April 1925 to coordinate the action of the current – still the majority, as had been demonstrated Como Conference in May 1924, where the left gained 41 votes, against the centre and right's 8 and 10 – in the face of the "Bolshevisation" being enforced on the party, according to the principles of Moscow. At first, Bordiga was in disagreement with this initiative; thereafter, he joined the action of comrades who, at risk of exclusion, however, had to dissolve the Committee of Understanding and face the Lyon Congress organisationally and politically marginalised. (See the book "Gramsci between Marxism and

Idealism" of Onorato Damen, [Prometeo Publishing], currently being translated into English). We can consider the Committee of Entente as the birth of the Italian left who opposed, not only nationally but also internationally, the first clear signs of the counter-revolution in Russia and the world. For a more detailed account of this see the CWO Pamphlet "Platform of the Committee of Intesa 1925", particularly its introduction.

[10] The term "New Party" was used by Palmiro Togliatti, general secretary of the Italian Communist Party (PCI), after landing at Salerno in 1944. With the change of name, Togliatti intended to root out once and for all the original internationalist roots of the class and revolutionary Communist Party of Italy PCd'I (which had never been completely compromised by Stalinism), inserting it into the national – and nationalistic – tradition through submission of the Italian proletariat to the requirements of the future "reconstruction" of capitalist Italy.

[11] The "Historic Compromise" is the name given to the political strategy launched by Enrico Berlinguer, general secretary of the PCI, after the fascist coup in Chile in 1973. Berlinguer, in the wake of the counter-revolutionary tradition of his "master" Togliatti, conceived a strong alliance between the "labour movement" and "healthy forces" of Catholic world, to overcome the difficult economic phase and "sort out the Country". Naturally, sacrifices for the "Country" would have to be paid in full by the working class. See also footnote [4] above.

[12] Umberto Terracini, a former member of Ordine Nuovo's Turin group, was a founding member of the Executive Committee of the PCd'I and co-editor, with Bordiga, of the fundamental Rome Theses which were presented at the Second Congress of the Party in Rome in 1922. He then supported the "centre" of the party in the struggle against the Left; arrested by the fascists, he spent many long years in prison. Having raised doubts about Stalinist policy and the bloody "purges" of the 1930s, he was marginalised by his own now-Stalinised comrades, who were detained with him. Returning to the PCI, after the war he contributed to the drafting of the new Constitution of the Italian Republic, in this way signalling his final transition to the other side of the barricade, against the revolution.

[13] *Programma Comunista* is the name of the periodical of the group which was headed by Bordiga, after the split of 1952. It began publishing as the new organ of the party which was referred to as the "International Communist Party". For some numbers, until the middle of 1952, the group, remained faithful to the theoretical positions and political principles of Bordiga, continued to publish an apocryphal *Battaglia Comunista*; in No. 7 of the latter, there was a bitter denunciation of "activism" to stigmatise that fraction of the party remained faithful to its congress deliberations and in a particular way to "Damenism"

"As with certain blood infections, which are caused by a lot of diseases, including those that the lunatic asylum can cure, activism is a disease of the labour movement that demands continual care ... activism brags that it can turn the wheel of history through shaking its backside in waltzes on an electoral symphony. It is an infantile disease of communism, but also matures wonderfully in care homes, where retirees of the labour movement vegetate. Requiescant in pace ... ".

It is with such a dismissive and authoritarian tone that Bordiga liquidated any personal relationship with Damen, comrade of so many battles and now considered mentally handicapped. In a short letter of March 28, 1952, he wrote:

"You know from past experience that my final and closing decisions are totalitarian and irrevocable. You have fallen into a state of infirmity, and if it was still possible to give you brotherly advice it would only be to give at least a few months rest to your brain. After that, I will ignore what you say to criticise, judge or worse threaten. Publish what you want: I only ask you do not send me anything, journals or anything else, and act as if you did not have my address. I have to learn from everywhere, not just teach, but in the material you put into circulation, there is not the slightest contribution, I will not look at anything more that reaches me."

[14] Again in March 1988 (*Programma Comunista* No. 3), the Bordigist epigones wrote about their positions "*defended by the Left* (lets be clear: only by "thoughts" of Bordiga passively waiting on events - Ed) in the second imperialist conflict, when we, to the shame of all democratist rhetoric, said in plain words that we wanted the victory of the Axis as the most favourable condition for the future path of the international class struggle".

Amadeo Bordiga Beyond the Myth and the Rhetoric (pages 21 to 30)

[15] The Italian Chamber of Deputies (parliament) is to be found on Montecitorio in Rome.

[16] Karl Kautsky (1854-1938) German Social Democrat, a former secretary of Engels, was the most widely known defender of the Second International. From 1909 though he lost confidence in the working class' ability to carry out the overthrow of capitalism and thus took a centrist position in opposition to the revolutionary wing of the Social Democratic Party (Mehring, Zetkin, Liebknecht, Luxemburg). In 1914, he did not oppose the Party majority who were in favour of Germany entering the war. His theoretical and political positions led to opportunism, a reformist minimum programme, and a "peaceful" conception of imperialism which led to his violent clash with Lenin (Kautsky criticised the dictatorship of Bolshevik power) because he considered him a renegade and denounced him as such (See Lenin's pamphlet: The Proletarian Revolution and the Renegade Kautsky).

[17] Giovanni Giolitti (1842-1928), President of the Council (i.e. Prime Minister) five times between 1892-1921. The strong man of Italy in the years before the First World War, he symbolised the access to power for the generation which had not taken part in the Risorgimento. After the factory occupations of the Red Two Years (1920-21) he allowed the Fascists 35 seats in parliament from his own right wing bloc thus opening the door to power for their repression of the working class.

[18] National Conference of the Communist Fraction of the PSI 28-9 November 1920.

[19] Founding Congress of the Communist Party of Italy (PC d'I) in January 1921.

[20] Theses approved at the Second Congress of the PC d'I in March 1921. See also footnote [12].

[21] Created in April 1925 to struggle against the Zinoviev-inspired Bolshevisation of the PCd'I. The declaration of the Committee of Intesa (Understanding or Alliance) was signed by Bordiga, Bruno Fortichiari, Onorato Damen, Francesca Grossi, Ugo Girone, Fortunato La Camera, Mario Lanfranchi, Mario Manfredi, Ottorino Perrone, Luigi Repossi, Carlo Venegoni who were the principal leaders of the PC d'I, all members of the historic left of the Party. It was dissolved on the injunction of the Comintern in July 1925. See also footnote [9].

[22] Palmiro Togliatti (1893-1964). A former Ordinovist he became the henchman of Stalin. Under the name Ercoli he was an executioner of the working class during the Spanish Civil War (1936-9). He became General Secretary of the PCd'I after Gramsci was arrested and sent to the islands off Sicily (where he joined Damen and Bordiga). He returned to Italy as head of the renamed Italian Communist Party (PCI) which he headed until his death in 1964. See also footnote [10].

[23] Giacomo Matteotti (1885-1924) secretary of the PSU (Unitary Socialist Party - a right wing split from the Socialist Party). He was assassinated in June 1924 by a Fascist group shortly after denouncing the Mussolini Government.

[24] On the 27 June 1924 the Matteotti assassination provoked a protest reaction (which took the name the Aventine Secession referring to the history of ancient Rome when the plebians revolted against the patrician Senate by taking themselves onto the Aventine Hill in 449 BC) by some deputies of the "democratic" opposition who refused to take their seats. For several weeks the Mussolini Government seemed on the point of collapse in the face of a wave of indignation across the country. Bordiga and the left communist tendency opposed this abstentionism. He demanded that the party struggle for the last time using "revolutionary parliamentarism". Repossi, a member of the left of the party returned to parliament to denounce Mussolini's cops in the name of the PCd'I. For the Italian Left if parliament was historically no longer an arm which the workers could use as in the Nineteenth Century here they were still a means to oppose all the factions of the capitalist class whether democrat or Fascist. For the Italian Left it was necessary to show that the only effective way to stop Fascism was to fight for the proletarian revolution.

[25] Italy was united in the nineteenth century under the Kingdom of Piedmont-Sardinia headed by the House of Savoy.

[26] Ruggiero Grieco (1893-1955). At first a member of the Abstentionist Fraction after Bolshevisation he became a Stalinist. Damen has had a memory lapse here. It was Repossi and not Grieco who returned to the Chamber of Deputies. Luigi Repossi (1882-1957) was elected a member of the Executive Committee of the PCd'I in 1921. He was expelled from the Party in 1929 as would Bordiga, Damen, and Fortichiari in the period 1930-33. After the war, with

Fortichiari he played an entryist role in the PCI of Togliatti. Bordiga never forgave him and refused to see him even on his deathbed.

[27] In 1952.

[28] Bordiga did not join the Internationalist Communist Party between 1944 and 1952 but did write the series of articles called "Sul filo di tempo" (On the thread of time) in the party theoretical journal *Prometeo*.

[29] In May 1924 at the clandestine Congress of Como of the PC d'I the Left still had an overwhelming majority over the right (Tasca) and centre (Gramsci). It was slowly removed from leadership of the PCd'I (between 1923-6) by bureaucratic measures with support of the Communist International and its emissaries, most notably Jules Humbert-Droz and Manuilsky. See also footnote [9].

[30] A policy of narrow horizons limited to legal reformism and permanent compromise with capital.

[31] Bordiga was a qualified engineer and always maintained an interest in what was scientific and rational.

[32] From his exclusion from the PCd'I in 1930 until his death in 1970.

[33] By "anti-demogogic" Damen meant the cult of personality around Stalin denounced by Khruschev in 1956.

[34] The Fraction of the International Communist Left which published *Bilan* and *Prometeo* (amongst other journals) in France and Belgium in the 1930s.

[35] The Internationalist Communist Party (founded 1943).

[36] Bordiga decided not to speak any more in the Central Committee after the Lyons Congress because he thought there was nothing more he could do there. He had been re-elected to the Central Committee against his will.

[37] Unable to meet in Italy the Third Congress of the PCd'I took place at Lyons (20-26 January 1926). In it the Left were defeated and isolated as a fraction in the PCd'I and the International. Gramsci achieved this by threatening the delegates who were paid party officials that they would lose their party jobs if they voted for the Left. The votes of absent delegates were counted for the Gramsci faction. Bordiga and Venegoni were threatened with expulsion if they did not take up their seats on the Central Committee to represent the Left. Bordiga was elected one of the delegates of the PCd'I to the Sixth Enlarged Executive of the Communist International (February-March 1926). For Bordiga's speech there see leftcom.org or https://

www.marxists.org/archive/bordiga/works/1926/comintern.htm. See also footnote [9].

[38] Umberto Terracini (1895-1983), Founded *Ordine Nuovo* with Gramsci. He was part of the first Executive Committee of the PCd'I in 1921 with Bordiga, Repossi, Fortichiari and Grieco who were all members of the abstentionist fraction. In 1947 he was behind an opposition within the PCI which the Communist Left at the time described as a purely personal attempt to replace Togliatti as leader. The letter of Bordiga to Terracini was sent on 4 March 1969. See also footnote [12].

Five Letters and an Outline of the Disagreement (pages 31 to 62)

[39] Damen is here responding to Bordiga's document "Theory and Action in Marxist Doctrine" which was published in the Internal Bulletin of the Internationalist Communist Party. It was an amended version of an "international address" Bordiga had made in April in Rome when Damen had been present. The article, including the graph Damen refers to, can be found in English at http://www.international-communist-party.org/English/Texts/51TheoAc/51TheoAc.htm

[40] Both Bordiga and Damen keeping referring to the "the state of Washington" thus to avoid confusion for US readers we have added D.C. where appropriate so as to make it clear that this is not the state in the North West corner of the USA. On the other hand no attempt has been made to alter the Italian habit of referring to "English" when they really mean "British" throughout the correspondence.

[41] Jacques de Palisse was a feudal lord who died at the battle of Pavia in 1525. His fame rests more though on the nonsense verses and songs written about him after his death. "If he wasn't dead he would still be alive" being the most famous. Bordiga here appears just to be saying "nonsense" again.

[42] "For the use of Onorio" i.e. for Damen's eyes only.

[43] There is a real place called Roccacannuccia in Puglia (about 15 miles south of Lecce) but it has no connection with the term used here. It is common practice to use it to refer sarcastically to nowhere in particular.

[44] American battleship then in the harbour in Naples, Bordiga's home town.

[45] Bordiga is here referring to his own series of writings published in Battaglia Comunista under the rubric of *Il Filo Del Tempo* (The Thread of Time).

[46] Name of a series of articles by Bordiga published in Prometeo in 1948-9

[47] More than once Bordiga uses the Italianised version of the French "dirigisme" or "state direction of the economy" – a policy which can be traced back to Napoleon I and which he

seems to see as a precursor of state capitalism.

[48] Bordiga means Petrograd which retained that name until Stalin re "baptised" it after Lenin's death in 1924.

[49] The Convention was the legislative body which, led by the Jacobins, dominated the French Revolution from 1792-4 and it was against this that the British Government originally declared the war (1793) which, with one brief respite (1802), continued until the final defeat of Napoleon in 1815. Discerning readers will not have failed to notice in this exchange that we have not altered the usage common to Italian of referring to everything British as "English".

[50] Damen means here the October Revolution of 1917

[51] And on this, enough.

On the Union Question (pages 63 to 67)

[52] One of the constant complaints that Damen makes about Bordiga was that he conducted much of his opposition to the PCInt in private correspondence to his known supporters (mainly Vercesi and Maffi) who then took up his arguments inside the Party.

[53] Giuseppe Di Vittorio (1892-1957) ex-anarcho-syndicalist; took the place of Ravazzoli in the union work of the PCI when the latter was thrown out of the P.C.d'I. as a Trotskyist (He was part of the New Opposition with Tresso and Leonetti, the so-called group of "Three"); during the liberation he was part of the Communist Party leadership. Elected secretary of the CGIL in 1945.

[54] Ottavio Pastore (1887-1965), became chief editor of the daily *L'Unità* in 1924.

[55] Ludovico D'Aragona, was secretary of the C.G.L., an organisation which he declared dissolved during WW1. He continued to be a leader of the C.G.L in the post-war period and had an important role in the factory occupation movement in Turin, signing the agreement with the bosses to return to work.

[56] Layer or strata, in French in the original.

[57] This comes from a letter-document sent to Bordiga with the intention of defining more precisely his points of agreement and disagreement on the union question.

[58] In March 1951 Damen and Bottaioli left the Executive Committee of the Internationalist Communist Party in which they were a minority. Giovanni Bottaioli "Butta" (1900-1959) was the child of farm labourers who joined the Italian Socialist Party and then adhered to its Communist Fraction in 1919. After several direct encounters with fascist thugs he was forced

to move to France in 1923 where he took up a trade as a plasterer. He was a militant of the Italian Communist Fraction abroad once crossing swords in a Communist cell with Maurice Thorez, future leader of the French Communist Party. Thorez, exasperated, threatened him with the words "Don't forget Jean I am a miner". Butta replied "Maurice, and don't forget I am a brickie". Rejecting the decision of Ottorino Perrone (Vercesi) to dissolve the Fraction at the start of the Second World War he formed a section of it in Marseilles with Aldo Lecci, Suzanne Voute and Marc Chirik in 1943. After exile in France, he returned to Cremona in 1945 where he became an executive member of the newly-formed Internationalist Communist Party and remained with Damen and its other founders in the split of 1952. His obituary was written by Luciano Stefanini ("Mauro") and can be found in *Battaglia Comunista* No 3 (April-May 1959)

[59] The First National Congress of the Internationalist Communist Party was held in Florence, from the 6-9 May, 1948. Following the national meeting in Turin, 1945, taking into account the inevitable existence of certain disagreements, and misunderstandings amongst the cadres of the Italian Left, after two decades of dispersion and isolation, the Congress approved a set of Theses which some members of the party accepted with open reservations. As the national and international situation worsened in an ever-more revolutionary sense, some symptoms of crisis appeared with the appearance of a tendency in the party leadership, of a pessimistic nature, if it can be put in that way, regarding the development of the political and organisational tasks which were being imposed. See the Pamphlets produced by Edizioni Prometeo – *The Process of formation and birth of the Internationalist Communist Party* and *The Internationalist Split of 1952*. We should make it clear that ever since this party had been created in 1943, there existed a tendency within it which sought to restrict its tasks, going so far as to deny the historical legitimacy of its very existence. According to them, the party should not have reappeared until after an overturning of the reactionary situation which characterised the post-Second World War period. There were those who advocated the construction of a fraction rather than a party, when the former had exhausted the reasons and tasks for which it was created in the twenties in the context of the centrist experience. With the passing of all worker parties to the side of the counter-revolution which had been confirmed in Russia, the problem of forming a new party became something necessary and urgent, even if only not to lose all the work that the fraction had done in those years. By way of a synthesis, here is the assessment made by Onorato Damen at the Turin Meeting and the Congress in Florence: *"For the proletariat to again become a revolutionary force it must be assisted, it must be helped so as to learn to recognise its enemies and be free from the influence of the workers' parties that have gone over to the counter-revolution. And it is up to the party to create in the heat of the fight the human class force which is called on to solve this crisis in a revolutionary way, otherwise it leads us to war. In this sense the party is revealed as the necessary theoretical, critical and organisational condition for this revolutionary solution: revolution, or war."*

[60] Workplace Committees (Comissioni interni) were set up in factories by the Fascist regime partly to get round the unions and partly to implement their corporatist ideology. They continued to exist under the new Republic.

[61] Alcide De Gasperi was the founder of the Christian Democratic Party and first post-war premier of Italy (with Togliatti as his deputy)

Crisis of Bordigism? Maybe, But Not a Crisis of the Italian Left (pages 74 to 81)

[62] Between late January and early February 1923, established a few months ago the fascist government, the police arrested most of the leaders of both the centre and the provinces of PCd'I., including Bordiga, making the operation of the Executive Committee impossible. They were accused of "conspiracy against the state." The Communist International took advantage of this to "advise" the Italian party to form a new leadership. At first Togliatti took over temporarily but later it fell directly on Gramsci. The control of the Comintern over the Italian party was growing.

[63] The Comintern or Communist International was founded in Moscow in March 1919 by the Russian Communists and a handful of delegates representing the few already formed communist parties and leftist groups. It was established that the number of national representatives were proportional to the number of members from each party, so that the USSR had a predominant weight in the decisions and policies of the Comintern line, especially after 1921, when gradually the national interests of Russia started appealing to the need to defend "the country of socialism".

[64] By this we think Damen means a kind of intellectual dilettanteism or trying to look clever for the sake of impressing others with their knowledge [Translators' note].

[65] In French in the original, it can be translated as "without qualification".

[66] The Workers Governments of Thuringia and Saxony saw the practical application of the disastrous formula of the "workers' government" (to which was later added the term "and peasant") adopted at the Fourth Congress of the Communist International (1922), a formula for which Bordiga demanded a "third-class funeral." In October 1923 the K.P.D. participated in the governments of the Länder of Saxony and Thuringia, led by "left" social democrats. This triggered a reaction from the central government, who with the support of national social democracy sent troops to disarm the communist "worker centurions" and put an end to this opportunist experience by military means. The KPD leadership, with the support of the IC, although the objective conditions were totally unfavourable, sparked the uprising planned in Hamburg anyway, which was inevitably defeated militarily due to the lack of mobilisation of most of the working class. This "German October" as it was called, signalled the eclipse of revolutionary hopes in Germany and the rest of Europe. For more see footnote [108].

[67] The National Meeting of the P.C.d 'I. was held in May 1924. The clandestine conference which brought together party leaders approved the resolutions proposed by the Left of Bordiga, who received 35 votes plus that of the Secretary of the Youth Federation, while the motion of Gramsci received 4 votes and that of the right-wing of Tasca 5.

[68] Flexibility. In French in the original.

From Dialectics to Sophism (pages 81 to 84)

[69] The original Italian word is "scarponi". Bordiga is here referring to his opponents (i.e. the majority) in the Internationalist Communist Party [Translators' note].

[70] The original term is "ballistica" [Translators' note].

The Irrational in the World of the Superstructure (pages 85 to 90)

[71] Giorgio Galli (born 1928) is a well-known historian and political commentator with many books to his credit including a history of the Italian Communist Party (PCI). He chaired the 2009 meeting which launched the Archive of our late comrade Mauro Stefanini (who died in 2005). See http://www.leftcom.org/en/adverts/2009-06-10/milano-archivio-mauro-stefanini

[72] The book is the 1971 version which was a much shorter version of the current work and entitled *Bordiga* with the subtitle *Value and Limitations of an Experience in the History of the "Italian Left"*.

[73] For the full context see page xx of the current publication

Axioms of Revolutionary Theory and Practice (pages 91 to 97)

[74] Title of the lecture that Bordiga gave in the Casa del Popolo, Rome, 24 February 1924.

[75] After the failure of the parliamentary opposition tactic of "the Aventine withdrawal", the Fascist government decreed the abolition of opposition parties and unions between 1925 -26, created a secret political police (OVRA) and a special tribunal for the Defence of the State, banned strikes and lock-outs and only recognised Fascist union.

[76] This English translation is taken from the Marxists Internet Archive and seems to differ quite substantially from the Italian used by Damen. For example, there is no mention of Trades Unions as "permanent organisations" in the Italian version. The bracketed inserted comment is by Damen.

[77] Taken from the CWO pamphlet *Platform of the Committee of Intesa 1925* subtitled *The start of the Italian Left's fight against Stalinism as Fascism increased its grip* pp. 18-19.

[78] Like all quotes from Bordiga in this book, this is our own translation. The English translation of *The Fundamental Theses of the Party* by the Bordigists themselves can be found at http://www.sinistra.net/lib/upt/compro/liqa/liqamcebue.html but it is obviously by someone whose first language was not English and we wish anyone luck in making sense of it.

[79] Damen is here referring to the internal organisation of the International Communist Party (Programma Comunista) which Bordiga and Maffi formed after the split with the Internationalist Communist Party in 1952. Apparently these "Unique Commissars" ran the individual sections of that party, transmitting to them the decisions of the Executive Committee.

The "Absolutes" of Neo-Idealism (pages 98 to 103)

[80] See footnotes 2 and 9

[81] The group Invariance led by Jacques Camatte split from Programma Comunista in 1966 (i.e. 4 years before Bordiga died). It took its title from one of Bordiga's first documents after the split with the Internationalist Communist Party, a set of 26 theses published in September 1952 as "The Historical Invariance of Marxism". See https://libcom.org/library/historical-invariance-marxism-amadeo-bordiga. As in so many issues Damen does not take issue with Bordiga, even if he finds his formulations vague but with his followers, "the epigones" who take Bordiga's ideas and then distort them into ridiculous positions. Camatte here was a classic. After splitting with Bordiga and Programma Comunista, Camatte maintained that "What is invariant, is the desire to rediscover the lost community" – by which he meant "primitive communities [where] human beings rule technology" as in the *gemeinwesen* of primitive communism which Marx talked about in the 1844 Manuscripts (see below). But he did not stop there and in the end he concluded that Marx too was wrong and that the "despotism of capital" actually produces a "collection of slaves of capital," rather than contending classes. The "invariance of Marxism" thus became the obliteration of its central tenet.

[82] Damen is referring here to the original International Communist Party founded by Bordiga and which publishes Programma Comunista.

[83] This translation is based on the version of *On James Mill* in David McLellan *Karl Marx: Selected Writings* p.115 except that where Damen has used the original German terms McLellan has omitted we have retained them.

[84] This translation from https://www.marxists.org/archive/marx/works/1844/manuscripts/comm.htm

[85] See footnote [75] above.

We Defend the Italian Left (pages 104 to 119)

[86] Damen means Bordiga here. Bordiga retired from political activity and refused all contact from 1926-45.

[87] This refers to the Hungarian workers rising against Stalinism in 1956 in which "workers'

councils" made their appearance before the movement was crushed by Russian tanks.

[88] Although he had no university degree Damen was a notable classicist so his writings are dotted with such references. Thespis was named by several sources, including Aristotle, as the first actor (i.e. one who took the identity of another). He sang the main part in dithyrambs whilst the chorus supported him ("helots" being slaves). He toured with all his costumes and props in a wagon hence the reference here. He gives us the name "thespian" for an actor.

[89] National Conference of the Communist Fraction of the PSI, November 1920.

[90] Daniel De Léon (1852-1914) played a prominent role in the foundation of the Socialist Workers' Party of America (SLP) and Industrial Workers of the World (IWW).

[91] Antonio Graziadei (1873-1953) became a P.C.d'I. executive member when Bordiga was arrested in February 1923 and before Bolshevisation consolidated the future group of Stalinists around Gramsci. Anselm Marabini (1865-1948) was an old maximalist who in 1921 formed part of the Central Committee of the P.C. of Italy.

[92] The Italian Communist Party (PCI) was formed under the leadership of Togliatti as a completely Stalinist party after the war. It dropped the old name of the Communist Party of Italy (PC d'I) as a symbol that it had abandoned any internationalist pretensions.

[93] *Iskra* (The Spark) was founded by Lenin in 1900 as a Marxist underground newspaper throughout Russia. Later, at the Second Congress of the RSDLP (Russian Social Democratic Labour Party), it became the organ of the party, under the leadership of Lenin, Julius Martov and Plekhanov Giorgi. Lenin left the editorshop in 1903, when *Iskra* became the organ of the Menshevik trend.

[94] The Second Congress of the RSDLP, held between London and Brussels in 1903, confirmed the support of the party majority for the left wing led by Lenin, who conceived the party as political vanguard, strictly disciplined and composed of professional revolutionaries, a scheme that suited existing conditions in Tsarist Russia.

[95] *Rabocheye Dyelo* (The Cause of Labour) was published between 1889 and 1902 . It adopted intermediate positions between economism and revolutionary social democracy. Lenin wrote in 1902: "*Rabocheye Dyelo* has become particularly important, historically if you will, as it expresses in the most clear and complete manner, not coherent economism, but the confusion and hesitation that characterise an entire period of the history of Russian Social Democracy."

[96] The newspaper *Youzhny Rabotchi* (The Worker of the South), published clandestinely between 1900 and 1903 was led by a group that, while condemning terrorism and economism and claiming that a mass revolutionary movement was required, proposed building the party based on the regional Social Democrats unions. At the Second Congress of 1903 it adopted a

centrist position.

[97] See also Footnote [62]. The campaign for "Bolshevisation" launched by the Communist International leaders in the years 1924-1925 with the purpose of subjecting all national sections to the discipline and directives of Moscow, replaced the territorial organisation which until then the PC of Italy maintained with factory cells. The Left, with Bordiga, condemned this "policy of manoeuvring and expedients" which actually went so far as to deny the centralisation of the communist parties. Indeed, the cells drowned internal party life by trapping the workers within the narrow confines of the factory, reinforcing the bureaucratic power of party officials divided into watertight compartments. Particularism and individualism were strengthened and corporatism and workerism ended up breaking the organic unity of the party while the Comintern gave intellectuals the monopoly of political authority.

You Cannot Build the Party Playing with Paradoxes (pages xx to yy)

[98] The comrades regrouped around the review "Parti de Classe" initially came out of a French group of the Bordigist International Communist Party which produced the review "Invariance" (see previous article) which we are talking about here and only later did they also break with "Invariance" to form the present group.

[99] Literally "in the manner of geometry". Damen here refers to the futile attempt to turn ideas into mathematically worked out axioms or theorems (following the principles of [Euclidian] geometry). The most famous example of this was Spinoza's attempt to systematise the thoughts of Descartes in this way but Damen always has Bordiga (or here Bordigism) in mind when he talks of this kind of mechanical thinking.

[100] See footnotes [62] and [97] above.

[101] Disputed question.

[102] Work of preliminary preparation before you can embark on a course of study. Here Damen uses it to talk of the period of work to prepare the party for the time when the working class has reached the point where it can no longer go on living under capitalism.

[103] Ottorino Perrone, also know as Vercesi was a leading member of the Fraction in Belgium and later the main supporter of Bordiga in his campaign to dissolve the Internationalist Communist Party. He was the main instigator of the dissolution of the Fraction on the eve of the Second World War on the grounds that as the proletariat no longer existed then neither could proletarian political organisations. It was this kind of abstract metaphysical position that became one of the hallmarks of Bordigism and which Damen fought all his political life. For more on Vercesi see Appendix 1 "The Fraction and Bordigism".

[104] In short, Bordiga.

[105] To which we can add the material fact that by registering and putting up candidates the PCInt got the right to speak on all platforms in every town square where they could directly confront the lies of the Stalinists. They continued thought to call for people not to vote. See the leaflet issued in 1948 "Don't Vote for Any Party" which can be read in English at http://www.leftcom.org/en/articles/2015-05-01/don-t-vote

[106] Painful or weak point.

[107] See footnote [102]

Bologna 1919 (pages 131 to 134)

[108] Damen is referring to the disastrous consequences of the KPD's (Communist Party of Germany) decision to apply the united front formula of joining a "workers' government" in Thuringia and Saxony in 1923. The policy of attempting to form 'workers governments' (later 'workers and peasant governments') was approved at the IV Congress of the Communist International (1922) as part of the wider united front policy aimed at maintaining Communist Party links with the masses. In 1923 the French occupation of the Ruhr and the infamous 'great inflation' provoked massive social strife. In a confused political framework (where 'national bolshevism' appeared to rival early Nazism) tens of thousands of workers went on strike against French requisitioning of food and other supplies. At Mulheim for example, workers took over the town hall, tried to form a workers council and their own militia. In August the Cuno government was forced to resign. As the situation became more polarised many workers turned away from the Social Democrats and looked to the KPD to give a political lead. The KPD leadership, however, typically swayed from one expedient to another. Having judged the situation unfavourable for workers to go on the offensive the KPD leadership under Brandler followed Russian advice and adopted a plan to join the left Social Democratic governments of Saxony and Thuringia. This, they knew, would provoke the national government, (headed by Ebert and the Social Democrats), to send in the army to which they planned to respond by calling a national general strike as the launch pad for a revolutionary insurrection. Of course the local Social Democrats reneged on the plan and the SPD as a whole refused to support a general strike. The central government duly sent in troops and the KPD leadership called off the action. News of this came too late for Hamburg where the local KPD attempted to launch the insurrection and fought on for three days against impossible odds. Thus ended the so-called 'German October', which signalled the eclipse of revolutionary hopes in Germany and elsewhere.

[109] Virgilio Verdaro (1885-1960) He joined the PSI in 1901. During the First World War he was accused of defeatism and sent into internal exile in Calabria. After the war contributed to Il Soviet and was an abstentionist delegate to the 1919 Bologna Congress. Present at the birth of the Communist Party of Italy, Livorno January 1921. Exiled to Russia in 1924 where his love of cats gave him the nickname 'Gatto Mammone'. He used this pseudonym in Belgium after he had fled from Russia in 1928, having been accused of Trotskyism. Part of the

communist left fraction, he was a key contributor to *Bilan* and *Prometeo*. His wife was pregnant and obliged to remain in Russia until just before the Second World War. Expelled from the Communist Party and sacked from her job, she existed in extreme poverty and her child died. At the outbreak of war Verdaro left Belgium and he and his wife went to Switzerland, his place of birth. He ended up joining the Socialist Party of Switzerland in 1943.

[110] Herman Gorter (1864-1927). 1897 joined the Social Democratic Workers Party (Netherlands). 1909, part of the Marxist left current associated with the newspaper, *De Tribune* which was expelled over their criticism of the corruption and opportunism of social democracy. Gorter joined those who went on to form the Social Democratic Party (SDP) which in the same year published Gorter's *Marxism and Revisionism*. Unlike some of the SDP leaders, Gorter argued that workers had no interest in supporting either side in the world war and in Imperialism, Social Democracy and World War he argued workers must oppose war by the fight for socialism. After the Russian Revolution (1918) the SDP changed its name to the Communist Party of Holland. Gorter himself joined the German Communist Party (KPD) before becoming part of the minority who were expelled for opposition to participation in parliament and the unions. They went on to form the German Communist Workers Party (KAPD) and Gorter became its most famous theorist with the publication, in 1920 of his '*Brief Reply to Comrade Lenin*' in response to Lenin's '*Left-wing Communism, An Infantile Disorder*'. After the Third Congress of the Comintern, the KAPD split with Gorter adhering to those who attempted to form a new International in the shape of the KAI (Communist Workers' International).

Anton Pannekoek (1873-1960). Like Gorter he was a leading figure in the anti-revisionist battle in the Netherlands before the First World War; editor of *De Tribune* from which the German-Dutch Left were known as the Tribunists. Opposed the war on a class basis and shared the political trajectory of Gorter although an even more prolific writer. He was famous for his elaboration of the ideas of council communism. However, it must be said that Pannekoek also argued that "the Party is the historically determined form of organisation which groups the more aware and prepared proletarians in struggle ... The communist party must have a well developed programmatic base, and must be organised and disciplined in its entirety from below, as a unified will". In his opposition to Stalinism, Pannekoek also recognised the Russian economic system as state capitalism.

Appendices 1-4 (pages 135 to 146)

[111] Ottorino Perrone (Vercesi) (1897-1957) was one of the most dominant but controversial figures in the history of the Communist Left. A founder member of the Communist Party of Italy in 1921 he was an early fighter against the degeneration of the Comintern (he was a signatory of the Platform of the Committee of Intesa 1925). After several arrests by the Fascist regime he emigrated first to France, from where he was expelled, then to Belgium in 1927. This meant he was not at Pantin (Paris) in 1928 for the foundation of the left fraction of the Communist Party of Italy. However he became principal editor with Gatto Mammone

(Virgilio Verdaro) of *Bilan* and *Prometeo*, the publications to the Belgian and French fractions of the internationalist communist left. He condemned the Spanish Civil War as imperialist from the start (criticised here by Damen for his "theoretically impeccable formula" or lack of recognition of the social revolution which accompanied its very early days) but later split the Fraction over his osciallations over the war. Right up until August 1939 Vercesi had maintained that the Munich Conference (September 1938) showed there would be no imperialist war and that the task of revolutionaries was to work to found a new internationalist communist party. However once war broke out he theorised the "social non-existence of the proletariat" and that it was defeated. It was the final blow to the Fraction which had already been suffering from divisions even before the war began. For the next four years many of the Fraction abroad tried to survive in clandestinity but several perished in the Nazi or Stalinist camps. Vercesi hid in Antwerp sheltered from the Gestapo by members of the Belgian Socialist Party. As a result of his apparent gratitude for this he made his next error of judgement which was to join an "Anti-fascist Committee" in Brussels as a representative of the Italian Red Cross. He later maintained this was for humanitarian purposes only but to many of his former comrades he looked to have simply sided with the victors in the imperialist war.

Meanwhile in Italy the strikes that broke out in the north in 1943 were the signal for the comrades like Damen, who had spent most of the previous decades in Fascist prisons etc, to form the Internationalist Communist Party (PCInt). Operating in clandestinity at first it recruited participants in the strike wave on a basic position of opposition to all sides in the war as imperialist. With the defeat of the Axis the Party could operate openly and many from the Fraction abroad returned to participate in the life of the new organisation. One who returned to Italy (but not to live there) was Vercesi. Not without vehement, even violent, opposition, his excuses re the Anti-fascist Committee in Brussels were accepted and he was allowed to join the Party in 1945. Damen makes clear that for all its weaknesses the Fraction abroad did help to take the analysis of the Italian Left forward and thus made a contribution to the eventual positions taken by the Internationalist Communist Party (on such things as unions, national liberation and even the imperialist nature of the USSR). However once the post-war wave of struggle began to subside the rapid rise of the PCInt began to slow. At this point (1948) doubts about the formation of the Party began to be raised by Bordiga. After almost two decades of non-participation in the life of the Italian Left (see Damen's comment about "this or that personality" in the article) he still did not join the Party but wrote a series of documents for it under the rubric "Sul filo di tempo" (On the thread of time). In these he did not openly attack the formation of the party but through correspondence with certain receptive party members (Vercesi in Belgium and Maffi in Milan) he began to propagandise against its existence. This eventually burst out into a split in 1951 when the Bordigists managed to outvote the original Party founders on the Executive Committee. Once again Vercesi had changed tack and became the spokesman first for the dissolution of the party then for the formation of the Bordigist alternative until his death in 1957. Ironically after calling for the dissolution of the party because the proletariat would not support it, both parts of the split increased their membership in the years that followed. It would take the full flowering of the post-war boom before this trend was reversed. The document here merely tries to highlight the incoherence and inconsistency of Vercesi's thinking by pointing to his better utterances.

[112] Karl Korsch (1886-1961) Studying in Britain before the First World War Korsch joined the Fabian Society however with the First World War his politics evolved dramatically. Back in Germany he was called up and at the end of the war elected by his regiment as delegate to the workers and soldiers councils. He joined the KPD at about the same time but like so many of its members did not leave when the comrades who would form the Communist Workers' Party (KAPD) were expelled in 1920 (see footnote [110] above). He did though support the Fischer-Maslow tendency until he was expelled with them in 1926. He founded the he formed the Entschiedene Linke (Determined Left) with Ernst Schwarz. It initially attracted 7,000 members, before recognising that its positions were identical to that of the KAPD which it entered in June 1927. Korsch made some telling contributions to Marxist theory, especially the notion of historical specificity in his *Marxism and Philosophy* (1923) and *Three Essays on Marxism* (1937 republished 1971) but by 1950 he was arguing that Marxism was no longer the basis for proletarian emancipation in his *Ten Theses on Marxism Today*. See also footnote [8]

[113] Ruth Fischer (1895-1961) One of the most controversial and colourful figures in the history of the Communist International. She was a founder of the Austrian Communist Party at the age of 24 and due to the support of Berlin's workers became a leading figure in the German Communist Party (KDP) by the age of 29. Her and her lifelong partner Arkady Maslow (1891-1941) pushed for a strategy of the "offensive" against the cautious leadership of Brandler. The failure of the November rising and the end of the cooperation with the SPD in Thuringia and Saxony in 1923 (see footnotes 66 and 108 above) brought the left of Fischer and Maslow to the leadership of the party, despite their known opposition to events both inside Russia and in the Comintern. In 1924 Korsch, a supporter of Fischer became editor of *Die Internationale* the KPD's theoretical journal. However when the Comintern delegate to the KPD Congress, Manuilsky, was heckled by delegates Stalin decided to act. Fischer and Maslow were replaced by his creature Thaelmann in 1926 and soon expelled from the KPD. They then set up the Leninbund which had 6,000. The Comintern offered to accept them back into the KPD and if they dissolved the Leninbund. Fischer and Maslow accepted the offer only for Moscow to refuse their applications to join. After Hitler came to power the two fled to France where they had several discussions with Trotsky but could not agree with his view that Russia was only a degenerated workers' state. For them a new revolution in the USSR was needed. After the Nazi invasion of France in 1940 they had to flee once again. Fischer managed to get to the USA via the services of Varian Fry in Marseilles but Maslow's visa application was refused so he fled to Cuba where he was mown down in a Havana street by a truck driven by Stalinists. After this Fischer became a CIA agent for 8 years and even came to believe that her elder brother had passed on the information to Stalin that led to Maslow's murder. She thus ended up denouncing both her brothers, Gerhard and Hans Eisler (the composer) to the House Un-American Activities Committee. She refused however to denounce communism when invited to do so by Richard Nixon. She denounced only Stalinism and after 1956 hoped that the "thaw" under Khruschev would lead to a new "democratic" communism. For more details see http://logosjournal.com/2012/spring-summer_kessler/

[114] Umberto Terracini (1895-1983). A lawyer by profession, Terracini, along with Angelo Tasca, Togliatti and Gramsci founded the journal Ordine Nuovo in 1919 and through this group became a founder member of the PCd'I. He was part of the group which supported the Bolshevisation of the Party and the manoeuvres against the Left leadership of Bordiga. From 1921-4 he represented (with Tasca) the Italian section on the Executive Committee of the Communist International. Returning to Italy he was imprisoned by Mussolini in 1928. Released in 1943 he resumed his support for Togliatti's PCI and became President of the Constituent Assembly which delivered the new constitution of the Italian Republic. A Deputy for the Communist Party until the 1970s and died as a Senator of the Italian Republic in 1983. Although sometimes seen as an unorthodox Stalinist (he rejected the Nazi-Soviet Pact of 1939 for example) he remained a loyal member of the PCI supporting, for example, the Soviet invasion of Hungary in 1956. See footnote [12] above.